150+ Real Ways
to Care for Yourself
While Caring for
Everyone Else

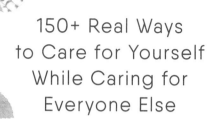

SELF-CARE
for
MOMS

SARA ROBINSON, MA

ADAMS MEDIA
NEW YORK   LONDON   TORONTO   SYDNEY   NEW DELHI

To all the moms: you are amazing, even when you feel like you're struggling. This book is for you.

Adams Media
An Imprint of Simon & Schuster, Inc.
57 Littlefield Street
Avon, Massachusetts 02322

First Adams Media hardcover edition April 2019

ADAMS MEDIA and colophon are trademarks of Simon & Schuster.

For information about special discounts for bulk purchases, please contact Simon & Schuster Special Sales at 1-866-506-1949 or business@simonandschuster.com.

The Simon & Schuster Speakers Bureau can bring authors to your live event. For more information or to book an event contact the Simon & Schuster Speakers Bureau at 1-866-248-3049 or visit our website at www.simonspeakers.com.

Interior design by Erin Alexander
Interior images © Getty Images/nicoolay/Ruskpp

Manufactured in the United States of America

10 9 8 7 6 5 4 3 2 1

Library of Congress Cataloging-in-Publication Data
Names: Robinson, Sara, (MA), author.
Title: Self-care for moms / Sara Robinson.
Description: Avon, Massachusetts: Adams Media, 2019.
Identifiers: LCCN 2018054479 | ISBN 9781507209905 (hc) | ISBN 9781507209912 (ebook)
Subjects: LCSH: Self-care, Health. | Mothers--Health and hygiene. | Mothers--Mental health.
Classification: LCC RA776.95 .R6253 2019 | DDC 613--dc23
LC record available at https://lccn.loc.gov/2018054479

ISBN 978-1-5072-0990-5
ISBN 978-1-5072-0991-2 (ebook)

Contents

Part 3

Introduction

Self-care. Your friends talk about it. You see articles online. It's necessary. You know that, but it's not always easy to make it happen. As a mom, you work hard to take care of so many things around you, including keeping people alive and helping them become good individuals who are ready to take on the world. Being a mom is exhausting, which makes taking care of yourself that much more important to your overall well-being. But it's also *really* hard to make self-care happen. Whether it's lack of time, busyness with kids, guilt over prioritizing yourself, or any other number of reasons, self-care for moms is easier said than done. But this book will change all that.

Throughout *Self-Care for Moms,* you'll find more than 150 self-care activities, organized by the amount of time you need to complete them and ranging from 5 minutes to a day or more. That's part of the beauty of this book. Once you start to think about self-care happening in shorter periods of time, and start implementing 5- and 15-minute activities, you'll see how that can have a big impact on how you think and feel, which can have a huge effect on how you handle everything else in your life. Chances are, your family will notice, too, which can encourage you and others to make the time for longer self-care activities.

These self-care activities will help you find new ways of taking care of yourself, and give you ideas about how you can include your kids in your self-care too (sometimes!). Trying out these new activities and learning more about self-care will also bring awareness to what you're already doing for yourself. It will help you be more intentional about including self-care in your already-packed schedule and help you create momentum and get better at planning, following through, and even seizing spontaneous moments just for you. And if you're really not sure how to make time for yourself or how to stay motivated to do that, you'll find a couple of chapters that help make these things easier as well.

This book was written for real moms: moms who are busy, moms with kids of varying ages, moms who sometimes struggle, moms who miss life pre-kids but wouldn't change a thing, and moms who know they need more self-care and want to feel better. It's for *all* moms, those who have the support of a partner and those who are doing it all solo. You *can* have more self-care in your life, starting with just 5 minutes at a time. The time to start is now!

Part 1

Making Self-Care a Daily Reality

Let's face it, *self-care* is a buzzword for moms, so much so that you may tune it out because you hear it so often! Who has the time and money for massages and spa days all the time? Fortunately, as nice as those activities are, that's not all that there is to self-care. In this part of the book, you'll learn what self-care *really* is, and how to make it happen on a regular basis. I know it's tempting to jump straight to the activities (they are great!), but start at the beginning and read these two chapters first to help set the stage for making self-care a reality for you.

Chapter 1

Let's Get Honest about Self-Care

This chapter will help you get ready to add more self-care into your life. You'll learn that self-care is more than the big, indulgent activities we tend to think about when we hear this term, and you'll discover the six categories of self-care that are essential to your overall well-being. You'll learn (or remember!) why self-care is so important and why you need to make it a priority. You'll build some awareness of what's getting in the way of making self-care a regular habit, and you'll find the inspiration you need to add more self-care into your life.

What Is Self-Care?

Self-care involves the activities, tasks, and practices that help you think and feel your best. And it can be such a loaded term for moms; maybe it makes you cringe because you know you're not doing enough. Or maybe the term brings up positive feelings, because you know you're doing a good job building self-care into your routine. You love self-care, you value it, and you want more of it! (Who doesn't?) Either way, self-care may sometimes feel difficult to prioritize, indulgent (like when you have an amazing massage or a deliciously decadent dessert), and tough to schedule. You are a mom, after all.

In fact, most of the objections to self-care come from feeling that there's not enough time, money, or both. We tend to think of self-care activities as time-consuming and/or expensive, but the reality is 1) you only need a minimum of 5 minutes at a time for self-care, and 2) self-care does not have to cost anything. Yes, you can choose activities or items that cost money, but as you'll see in Part 2, there are many self-care activities that cost nothing. It's all about the intention behind the activity.

And as for the thought that self-care has to feel indulgent, that is nice, but there is much more to self-care than that. There are actually six main types of self-care to know about, and you'll want to fit each type into your schedule.

Emotional Self-Care

Emotional self-care is about taking time for your emotions, participating in activities that create positive feelings, and also dealing with negative emotions. This means that part of self-care is dealing with the hard stuff. As a mom, you might not always be focused on your own emotions, because you're working hard to deal with everyone else's. But by ignoring your emotions or thinking that they'll handle themselves, you probably don't deal with #momlife as well as you should. Activities that fulfill your emotional self-care needs include taking the time to watch a movie you love, going for a walk outside, or possibly talking with a therapist.

Mental Self-Care

Mental self-care is taking care of your state of mind, doing something intellectually stimulating, or working to create positive thoughts. If we're not feeling stimulated or mentally engaged, it can be a recipe for disaster. You may find that you're more likely to take your frustrations out on your kids and those around you. As rewarding as being a mom is, that's not always enough mental stimulation, and you know that parenting can be mentally exhausting, and challenging. This is why mental self-care is a critical area of self-care to include in your regular routine. For example, journaling, reflecting on what you're grateful for, or doing a puzzle all help to take care of your mental state.

Physical Self-Care

Physical self-care is all about taking care of your body and involves things like working out, drinking plenty of water, and making sure to take care of essential doctors' appointments. This is a category that seems to be a challenge for moms because we often put ourselves last, and it can be hard to justify taking the time or spending the money for a gym membership or classes. But you need to prioritize your physical health, just like you do for the rest of your family.

Practical Self-Care

Practical self-care is often overlooked because it includes everyday tasks. However, cleaning your house, scheduling doctors' appointments, and organizing your family's calendar can be considered self-care too. Chances are, your life is already filled with *lots* of practical self-care, but you look at these things as chores and to-do lists. Instead, understand that these tasks are not only critical to the functioning of your family, but it's also beneficial for you when you complete them.

Social Self-Care

Social self-care is all about making time in your life for your friends, family, and loved ones. Making sure you maintain connections with others is important for everyone, but especially for moms. Your "free time" often gets filled up with kids' activities, and though you may socialize during those times, it's critical to make sure you also spend time with the people who are important to you. Social self-care can include meals and outings with friends and family, but it can also include quicker moments of connection, like calling a friend or grabbing a quick coffee. Even for introverts and exhausted moms, social self-care can't be overlooked.

Spiritual Self-Care

Spiritual self-care varies depending on your beliefs. It can mean going to church, praying, or reading religious materials, but it can also include meditation, connecting with nature, or any other activity that feeds your soul. Taking care of your spirit and soul is another key area of self-care. Busyness may lead to less time than you'd like to be spiritual, or you may feel that the family should do this together, but don't let barriers like those get in *your* way of meeting *your* spiritual needs.

As you can probably see, with a broader idea of what self-care *is*, there are so many options for what you can do that helps you take care of yourself, and one self-care activity can address more than one self-care need. Hopefully, now that you have a better understanding of self-care, you're already feeling more inspired to make it happen. But why is self-care so important? Why do you need to make it a priority in your life?

Why Prioritize Self-Care?

Even though you may not like to talk about it, being a mom is hard. Not always, and not every day, but it *is* difficult. And while it's also amazingly rewarding, because you have a lot on your plate, it's easy to put everyone else's needs before your own. But you deserve more.

No matter what your situation or circumstances, self-care is a critical key to your happiness and overall well-being. Self-care helps you function better—both mentally and physically—and, when you are at your best, you can do better in all areas of your life. Without it, you run the risk of getting run-down, having your negative emotions spill over into your interactions with family and friends, and experiencing some *mom guilt*. But when you're happy and well taken care of, you set the stage for the other areas of your life to function well, including caring for your kids.

Convinced yet? For your own good as well as the good of your kids and the larger family unit, your work, and any other responsibilities you have, you need to practice self-care—consistently, with intention, and without feeling bad about it.

What's Stopping You?

What gets in the way of your self-care? Make a list. You'll probably come up with the usual reasons: not enough time or money, your kids need you, your schedule is packed, or you don't have the energy. And, if you're a single mom, you may feel these things even more intensely. How are you going to find the time for yourself when you're the one taking care of everything and everyone without the support of a partner? But no matter what your situation, the reality is that *you* are stopping yourself from making self-care happen. You're making excuses, you're prioritizing other people and other things, and you're not being intentional with your time. It's okay. We all do it, but you can change. You just need to do a little planning.

Chapter 2

Plan for Your Self-Care

Now that you have a better understanding of what self-care is and why it should be a priority, let's get real for a second—making the time for self-care can feel impossible! Chapter 2 will help you with that. Here you'll learn how to make self-care happen regularly with time-management tips and strategies like scheduling self-care and including your kids in your activities. The chapter wraps up with how this book is organized, and then you'll be ready for Parts 2 and 3, which include more than 150 self-care activities for you to try.

Make Time for Self-Care

One of the biggest barriers to self-care is time. There just doesn't seem to be enough of it. Yes, life is busy, but there *is* time. You may need to find it, or make it, but it's there. You know your life; you know what's realistic. But chances are good that you're wasting time throughout the day or week that, with better organization and time management, could be shifted to self-care. Remember that the ages, number, and needs of your children will influence how and when you can do your self-care. Sometimes your life circumstances will make prioritizing yourself difficult, but that likely means that self-care is even more important for you. Let's take a look at how to make time for self-care.

Rethink Your Time

One of the best time-management strategies to help make self-care a habit comes from Laura Vanderkam, an expert on time-management. She suggests that you look at a week as 168 hours, rather than 24 hours a day. With *only* 24 hours, it is hard to think about fitting in *one more thing* like self-care, but when you shift your perspective and realize that you have 168 hours every week, you see how much time you have. For example, with 168 hours, even if you spend 40 hours at work, 10 hours commuting, 49 hours sleeping (and let's face it, that might be a good week!), 10 hours at kids' activities, 5 hours at other weekly commitments, and 5 hours dealing with meals, you still end up having 49 hours left to fill! Forty-nine hours. Okay, you're probably doing other necessary things during some of that time, but you get the point. You *can* fit in self-care. You just need to start thinking about time differently, fitting self-care into your calendar, and using your time intentionally and with purpose. You can also get creative about how you fit in self-care, as you'll see with some of these activities. (For example, how about listening to an audiobook while you do the laundry? A dreaded chore is now self-care!)

Schedule Your Self-Care

Once you realize that you *do* have the time, insert self-care in some of those time slots. Look at your existing routines to see where you can add in self-care activities. It can be as simple as lighting candles in the morning, having a book in your purse to read while you wait at pick-up, or adding music to your end-of-day chores. Look at where you can take 15, 30, or even 60 minutes during the week. If you'd ideally like to have an hour to work out but find that's not realistic, don't give up. Plan a 30-minute workout instead.

For any self-care option that will take longer than 5 minutes, it's helpful to schedule an appointment with yourself, like you would for your kids' lessons and activities. You're more likely to make self-care happen when you've got a date with yourself, on your calendar. It's useful to get in the habit of setting aside time each week to plan your self-care, not only for the week, but also looking long-term to see where you can fit in longer activities.

Let Others Help

Being committed to your own self-care is an important first step, but you're a mom. There are many people who can derail your efforts without even meaning to! So as you begin this journey, hold a self-care family meeting as suggested in Chapter 6 to help get everyone on the same page.

Another way to reinforce your commitment to yourself is to encourage people around you to give you gifts for self-care. When your loved ones ask you what you want for your birthday, Mother's Day, or other holidays, request things like gift certificates for services you'd like to enjoy, books you want to read, a gift certificate for a house cleaning service, or simply their time. Childcare is one of the biggest challenges for moms, so consider asking people you trust to help with your kids and look into other childcare options, like sitters or having older kids help with younger kids, so you can make self-care a habit.

Be Spontaneous

Though you want to plan ahead for your week and month by making appointments with yourself, it's also important to remember that self-care can (and should) be spontaneous at times. Fit self-care into small pockets of time when you notice them, such as when your kids are putting on their shoes and getting backpacks. Instead of bugging them to get going, step away from the situation and do a quick self-care activity like repeating affirmations, listening to a song that picks you up, or walking outside and just breathing.

Include Your Kids

Yes, self-care is about you, and it's often important to get away from your responsibilities to accomplish it, but that's not always realistic, especially if you have young kids. Also, it's important to set a positive example for your kids by letting them see you take care of yourself. Throughout the book you'll find suggestions for when and how to include your kids in your self-care activities. Take the time for yourself whenever you can, but don't stop yourself from doing self-care simply because the kids are present. You might need to be creative about how the activity happens, or choose a kid-friendly activity, but kids shouldn't be a total obstacle to self-care. And, as your kids get older, they may enjoy the same self-care activities as you, which makes for great bonding opportunities before they leave the nest.

Multitask

Moms are great at multitasking. You can drive a car, open a snack, pick up something someone dropped, *and* hold a conversation all at the same time. You're pretty impressive. But multitasking has its limits. And generally, when it comes to self-care, you want to be fully present and immersed in your self-care activities to get the most from them. Of course, there are exceptions. Adding self-care to tasks that don't require your full attention can be very beneficial, such as listening to a podcast while you clean, listening to music while you watch your kids' lesson(s), or doing a craft while you watch TV. This sort of multitasking allows you to add a self-care element to an everyday chore and can help you move through your day in a better mental and emotional space.

How to Use This Book

So you see, you *do* have time for self-care. You just have to figure out how to fill that time with self-care activities that are tailored for you and the time you have available—and that's where the activities in Parts 2 and 3 come in.

Chapter 3 covers activities that require only 5 minutes of your time. You can do these spontaneously, or plan them into parts of your daily routine. As a mom, taking just 5 minutes for yourself a few times a day can really help you reset, regroup, and stay more grounded, especially if you notice things getting hectic. When you look at these quick-and-easy self-care suggestions, it's important to understand that self-care is not *just* big activities. Those activities are amazing (and there are two chapters dedicated to activities that take a couple hours or more), but the reality is, you only need a few minutes at a time.

As amazing as 5 minutes of self-care can be, the more self-care you can fit into your life, the better you'll feel. And who doesn't want more time for themselves? In Chapters 4–6 you'll find activities that will take as little as 15 minutes and some that take up to an hour. These longer activities are great for getting engrossed in an activity and focusing more on you. Then, in Chapter 7, you'll find activities that take 2–4 hours to complete. These longer activities give you more time for yourself, and often allow you to meet various self-care needs with one outing.

After you read this book, and make a plan, hopefully you'll find that your monthly calendar has many 5-minute activities, quite a few 15-minute activities, and then 30-minute and 1-hour activities sprinkled in. Fitting in a once-a-month activity that takes 2–4 hours would be amazing, but if it's less often, that's okay too. Get these longer activities on the calendar where you can, and then go even bigger. Set a goal to have a full day or more all to yourself, using the activities in Chapter 8. Once a year would be great; every three to six months is even better. Don't judge yourself by how much time you have to work with; simply make the most of what you have, and strategize about how to get the amount of time you want and need.

But no matter how much time you have available, remember that you are worth it and that the activities in Part 2 are activities that you *can* incorporate into your life and routine. Let's get to it!

Part 2
. . . .
Everyday Self-Care Activities

As moms, we need to stop making excuses that there's not enough time for self-care, or that it's something "special" that only happens infrequently. Instead, make the mental shift that self-care is necessary—it helps you be a better woman and a better mom—and commit to practicing it every day. If that feels unrealistic, you might still be thinking that you need a lot of time for self-care. But while it's nice to have *hours* to yourself (you'll learn how to spend those hours in Part 3), that's not the only way to make self-care happen. And thank goodness, because as a mom, you're busy!

In the chapters in this part you'll find a variety of powerful self-care activities you can do in just 5, 15, 30, and 60 minutes, which means you can definitely make self-care happen on a daily basis. No more excuses! And while finding 30 minutes or an hour daily may not always work, get creative. Aim to add in those activities once or twice (or more) during your week. You're worth it!

Chapter 3

5-Minute Activities

Five minutes may not seem like a lot of time, but you'll be amazed at what this time can do for you, especially when you make these brief activities a regular part of your day. You'll notice that many of the activities on this list are about emotional self-care and help to create a positive mood. As a mom, this is critical! You know that when you're in a good mood, everyone else is more likely to be too. Many of these activities are also about mental self-care, because when you're thinking positively, it has a ripple effect in all that you do and in your interactions with others.

The idea with these short, but impactful, activities is that you build them into your regular routine. Start the day with one activity (or more if you have time), and add others into the pockets of time that you create throughout the day and week. Do them spontaneously as well. These short bursts of self-care are perfect for when you might normally scroll mindlessly on your phone, when you're standing around waiting for someone (that happens a lot!), or when you begin to feel overwhelmed. Don't underestimate the power of 5 minutes. While it shouldn't be the only self-care you do, we all can find 5 minutes *at least* once in our day.

Call a Friend

A text is a quick way to connect with people and get the information you need. Because of the ease of texting, most of us have gotten away from calling people. In fact, it's easy to be annoyed when the phone rings. But without this old-school form of communication, we miss out on emotional connection with others. It's important to hear the voice of someone you care about and communicate in real time. Calling may feel hard to do, especially if you have young kids chatting (okay, yelling) in the background, but your friends will understand. You can even text someone first to see if they're available to chat.

Try making your call when your kids are engaged in an activity, or make the call in the car (if you can go hands-free) during your morning commute or after drop-off when your friend might be in the car too, or while you're prepping dinner. Consider starting a regular routine where, every day at the same time, you call your friends to say hi and see how they're doing. Connecting with others is a fundamental need, and having adult connection should be a regular part of your day and week. Work to build in social and emotional self-care with quick phone calls to friends and family.

Choose a Theme Song

This activity is *not* about putting on "Let It Go" (or whatever song your kids love) for the millionth time. No, this is about finding a song *you* love. What's the song that, if you played it on repeat, would make you just as happy on the fiftieth play as the first? What's the song that picks you up, makes you want to move, and helps you feel good? If you were in a movie, strutting down the street, feeling confident and happy, what would be playing in the background? That's *your* song. Music can change your emotions, create a positive mood, and help to improve your thoughts.

Once you know what your song is, play it any time you need emotional self-care or a pick-me-up. In addition to those moments, add your song into your daily routine. For example, turn it on first thing in the morning or listen on your phone while you're in line (for coffee, a prescription, ordering lunch, etc.). You can also have quick dance parties during the day, either on your own or with the kids (you may need a clean version of your song for this part!). Dancing to your favorite song on your own can be a great way to release negativity and frustration, so imagine what would happen if you invited your kids to join in (your tweens and teens may groan at you, but keep inviting them to join the fun). Add in a few daily dance parties, and you'll be getting some physical self-care too!

Practice Mindfulness

Mindfulness is the act of being in the moment, being aware, and taking note of how you're thinking and feeling. The idea is to create some space between the thoughts you have, the feelings you experience, and the way you react, without judging yourself—which is a great way to practice both mental and emotional self-care. For example, if your child spills milk after you asked him to be careful, your usual reaction might be to yell. When you act in a mindful way, you pause and observe, labeling your thoughts and what's happening. Internally, you might think, *He spilled milk. I'm feeling angry because I asked him to be careful.* When you create this space and are nonjudgmental about your thoughts and feelings, you're being mindful. Then you're able to more calmly respond to the situation by, for example, reminding your son that this is why you asked him to be careful and asking him to help you clean up.

For this 5-minute activity sit quietly, observing and experiencing your surroundings, and focus on your breathing. If thoughts come into your head, label them the way you saw in the spilled milk example, then go back to focusing on your breathing. After 5 minutes you can continue with your day. You may feel calmer, but the impact will increase the more you practice mindfulness. When you repeat this type of self-care consistently, you'll start to notice that you react to situations in a way that's calmer and more controlled, which is better for everyone.

Apply Great-Smelling Body Lotion

How many days do you look at your skin and think, *Ugh, so dry* or *I miss that youthful glow.* Chances are your skin needs some good hydration, and applying lotion is a great self-care option to help with this. As simple as this is, moisturizing is one of those steps that moms often end up skipping. How often have you rushed through a shower, grabbed the lotion, and then stopped because someone needed you? Probably too many times to count, no matter what the ages of your kids. For this self-care activity just pick your favorite lotion, and take the time to massage it into your skin. Do your whole body, savoring the physical sensations.

Applying lotion can also be an exercise in mindfulness. Pay attention to the sensations you're experiencing, and stay present in the moment. By focusing on what you're doing, you can clear your mind, even if it's for only 5 minutes at a time. Though you can do this activity with any lotion, a lotion with a scent you enjoy is best, so that the effects of the activity last beyond 5 minutes. The fragrance will remain on your skin and can help create positive emotions after this self-care activity is complete.

Delete Emails

We are all on way too many email lists. We get coupons for stores we went to once, and we're on mailing lists we don't remember signing up for. This results in hundreds of extra emails coming to your inbox each week, which can be overwhelming and distracting—even though most of them are junk. Though deleting emails may seem like a chore, this practical self-care can also have a direct, positive impact on your mood and mental state.

If you're starting with a *huge* number of emails, you may simply want to delete them all. Ideally you can select many emails at a time, without having to open them, and wipe them away. If this feels stressful, like you might miss something important, start with the oldest emails and look for any subject lines that say "coupon" or "sale." Those are expired; get rid of them. Open others if you must, but focus on deleting, and keep only what is needed.

It may take several days, or longer, to get the emails in your inbox to a manageable number that doesn't stress you out when you see it. It may not be realistic to delete them all (you may have emails that you need to reply to later), but working to get your inbox under control is important. Ideally, as you get a better handle on your emails, your 5 minutes can be spent removing yourself from mailing lists you don't want to be on rather than simply deleting.

Create (and Use!) a 5-Minute Makeup Routine

It seems like most moms have had the experience of looking in the mirror and thinking, *When's the last time I put on makeup?* or *I went out of the house without makeup again?!* It's so easy to focus on getting everyone else's needs met that we forget about or forgo putting the time into our own. And, when it comes to makeup, it's too easy to say, "I don't have enough time." But you do! While it would be nice to have as much time as you'd like to spend on your makeup, coming up with a 5-minute routine is critical for moms. Yes, you're beautiful without makeup, but let's face it, most of us feel just a little bit better when we accentuate our beauty (and hide those dark circles. Thanks, kids!).

Prioritize yourself and give this routine a try: apply moisturizer with sunscreen (tinted, if you prefer), under-eye concealer, blush, one coat of mascara, and something on your lips (gloss, lipstick, or any lip balm works great!). Then spritz yourself with perfume or body spray if you'd like. It's quick. It's simple. And you can add or take away based on how much time you have and how long each part takes. It's amazing that blush and mascara can be mental and emotional self-care, but they are! You can even create a bag of makeup essentials for your purse or car so that if you're running late, you can fit in this 5-minute self-care somewhere else in your day.

Savor a Piece of Fruit

Fruit is nature's candy. How many times have you said that to your kids? (If you haven't, you will!) But in all seriousness, fruit is an important way to get the essential vitamins and nutrients you need while enjoying something that tastes good. When you visit the grocery store, be sure to pick up a variety of fruit. Go for what's in season and fresh. Purchase fruit that *you* love, not only what your kids will eat.

When you get home, place fruit like apples, bananas, and pears (anything that can be left out) in a bowl, prominently displayed in your kitchen. This will encourage you and your kids to snack freely, and can act as a reminder to partake in this self-care activity. If you've purchased anything that needs to be cut up, make the time to do that after shopping so that when it's time for a snack, everything is ready for you. Sit and savor your fruit, enjoying each bite and really experiencing the flavors. Make this a slow, intentional, and quiet activity to get the most benefit out of this self-care option.

Make Your Bed

Not everyone cares if their bed is made. After all, you're getting back in it later in the day. And before that happens, your bed may be transformed into a fort, a wrestling ring, or a gymnastics mat, so it can seem pointless to spend time making it look nice. That said, starting the day by making your bed can lead to a feeling of accomplishment and can help to create a tidier, more put-together look in your room, which may help you feel calmer and more in control. Don't believe making your bed can do all that? If you're in the camp of not caring about your bed being made, try making your bed a couple of times and see if it changes anything for you. Too much work? Start with making the comforter look nice while ignoring the sheets underneath, and see how that makes you feel. If you already make the bed every day, try adding a pop of color with a new throw pillow or changing the comforter for something that makes you feel good. And keep in mind that this quick task isn't only self-care for you; it can also create a positive example for your kids.

Diffuse Essential Oils

Essential oils (EOs) are aromatic compounds extracted from various parts of plants and natural botanicals. They are typically bought as single scents, such as lavender or peppermint, and each EO brand will have signature blends you can add to your self-care routines. There are many ways to use essential oils, but one quick and effective way is to add five to eight drops of your chosen oil(s) into a diffuser created specifically for EOs. By adding your chosen oil(s) to the water in your diffuser, you distribute the molecules through the air, allowing you to experience the various benefits of the EOs. And one of the great benefits of diffusing EOs is that it can be done daily, creating not only a pleasant scent in your home but also mental and emotional self-care for everyone in your family.

Individual oils and different blends can create emotional and mental benefits. For example, frankincense, bergamot, and lavender help you feel calmer and more grounded, while orange, grapefruit, and peppermint are energizing and uplifting. You can even experience mental clarity and relieve stress by using rosemary, eucalyptus, and lemongrass. Use one, two, or three of the suggested oils as needed, and add other EOs to your collection to enjoy other self-care benefits.

Do 5-Minute Yoga

Yoga is a physical practice that is also a form of moving meditation. Adding a 5-minute yoga routine to the start or end of your day can ensure that you get consistent mental and physical self-care, and it's been shown to have calming effects for adults and children of all ages. Consider inviting your family to join you!

In just 5 minutes, three yoga poses held for approximately 90 seconds each can leave you feeling strong, grounded, and calm. Kneel on the floor, using a mat or rug under you for comfort. Sit back on your heels, then reach your hands out in front of you and bend your body over so your chest is flat on your upper thighs: this is child's pose with arms extended. After 90 seconds, slowly move to downward dog by keeping your hands flat on the floor, straightening your legs, and lifting your hips up. Ideally, your feet will be flat on the floor, and your legs and arms will be straight (like an upside down "V"). Hold this pose for 90 seconds, then walk your feet in to meet your hands, and slowly stand up. Finish with a standing mountain pose, feet hip-width apart with your hands resting on your chest in prayer position. Check online for videos showing the correct body positions. Be aware of your breathing as you complete your routine; refocus on your breathing if you become distracted. Be mindful of the experience, not on how well you're doing.

Add Flowers to Your Home

For moms, flowers often come for special occasions, but why not give every day a burst of color and happiness? Get in the habit of picking up an inexpensive bouquet on your weekly shopping trip (many stores have $5 bouquets), or cut flowers from your backyard. Arrange the flowers in a vase or in multiple vases if you prefer, and place them in spaces where you'll see them often but that are also out of the way of your kids. Remember, toddlers can usually reach further than you think they can, and older kids still throw balls in the house even when you remind them not to. Put the flowers on your bedside table to help make your room more of a personal sanctuary, or set them in a family space for all to enjoy.

This is easy self-care, because you're already out shopping. It only takes an extra minute or so to walk to the floral section and pick out the bouquet, and only a couple minutes more at home to put them in a vase. But the emotional self-care benefits can last for days…hopefully until your next trip to the store, when you can pick up another bouquet. If finances are tight but you like the idea of fresh flowers, ask the florist for a small bouquet of carnations and baby's breath, or replace one unnecessary grocery item with some flowers. For example, don't let your kids throw in two boxes of sugary cereal; they can have one, and you can have your self-care!

Drink Your Water

Staying hydrated is important to your overall physical self-care and will help all parts of your body function more effectively, including your brain. Take 5 minutes to fill up a water bottle to help you get the daily hydration you need. It's recommended that women drink at least 72 ounces (9 cups) of water a day. If you're pregnant, aim for 80 ounces (10 cups), and if you're nursing, the goal is 104 ounces (13 cups). Keep in mind that some of your fluid intake will come from the food you eat, but much of it will need to come from drinking water.

Set yourself up for optimal hydration by getting a reusable bottle that you like; go bigger than 8 ounces if you can, and fill it up at the start of the day. Try to find a bottle that will fit in the cup holder in your car, so that it travels easily. If you work out of the house, consider having a water bottle that stays at work, rather than having to remember to bring it back and forth, and if you're eating out during the day, ask for a glass of water with your meal to continue the hydration. Consider setting an alarm for midday to check on your progress…and to refill your bottle. Use dinnertime as another reminder to refill your water bottle again, and keep drinking.

Light a Candle and Breathe

If you're having trouble focusing or centering yourself, you may find it helpful to light a candle and take 5 minutes to just breathe. To begin this mental and emotional self-care, find a comfortable place where you'll be able to sit and breathe, uninterrupted. You may need to do this while your kids are still sleeping, or while they're engaged in play, homework, or screen time. This activity is most impactful with a scented candle, as the aroma can help boost your mood. Light the candle and get comfortable in your seat; lie down if you prefer. Focus on your breathing, inhaling slowly and then exhaling slowly. Most people find it comfortable to inhale through their nose and then exhale deeply through their mouth. Do your best to focus on your breathing. Close your eyes if you like, and zone out. The aim is to clear your mind.

This can be a challenge, especially the first few times you do it. If you find your mind wandering, add counting to your breathing to help you focus. For example, breathe in and count to six, then breathe out and count to eight. You might also find that you can focus longer if you watch the flame of the candle—just be sure to blow it out when you're done. Or continue to let the candle burn after this activity is complete; the scent can continue to boost your mood and may also act as a reminder to breathe and stay calm.

Do a Power Pose

Your body language influences both how you feel about yourself and how others view you. So it's useful to be aware of the message that you're sending (to yourself and others), and adjust your body language as needed to positively affect your mental and emotional state. One way to alter your body language is to strike a "power pose," a body position where you make yourself big. Standing, put your hands up in the air, or if you're sitting in a chair, spread out. Think legs apart, arms out wide. Essentially, you want to take up as much space as you can and hold that pose for 2 minutes.

One power pose is the "Wonder Woman" pose, where you stand with your feet hip-width apart and you're your hands on your hips. In the 2 minutes that you hold this pose, research has shown that your testosterone levels will increase and your cortisol levels will decrease. These hormonal changes will help you feel more confident and comfortable, and your stress level will decline. Isn't that amazing? Use this self-care activity any time you need a pick-me-up, when you're walking into a stressful situation, or when you feel like you lack power. Power posing can be done in private, and can be taught to (and done with) your kids so that they also learn about creating their own power from within.

Practice Gratitude

Practicing gratitude is an intentional focus and reflection on what you appreciate, big things and small. As a mom, you have *so much* to be thankful for, but that can easily get lost in the daily grind. This makes it all the more important for you to take the time to practice gratitude on a regular basis. Not only is it important mental and emotional self-care, but it also allows you to be present in the moment. Take the time to reflect on what you are grateful for; perhaps start a gratitude journal and write down what you appreciate. Obvious choices are your family, friends, health, and home, but try to get more specific. For example, you're grateful that your arms (and back!) are strong enough to carry your ever-growing toddler. You're thankful that your partner always takes the trash cans to the curb. You appreciate that your teens have taken an interest in helping others—you get the point!

Challenge yourself to be grateful even in the difficult parts of life. When you find gratitude in the tough moments and challenges, you can get through them more easily. When tough times are over, we often see the positives that came of the situation, or we're thankful we had the experience. But looking for something to be grateful for *in* a challenging moment can actually make the experience less stressful while it's happening.

Eat a Piece of Chocolate (or Your Favorite Candy)

You might be aware of the notion that if women want to practice self-care, all we need to do is indulge in a square of dark chocolate. Sounds delicious, but is it really true? Yes! Having some chocolate, your favorite candy, or any special, sweet treat can absolutely be self-care. But this shouldn't be your only self-care, especially since you might see your weight and blood sugar rise if you indulge too often.

Keep in mind that this self-care activity isn't about wolfing down a pack of Skittles or powering through a Snickers as you rush about your day. This is about taking the time to enjoy the experience of eating the candy. It's important to be deliberate and mindful about this time, and your treat. Savor each bite, noticing the flavor and texture, and do so without guilt. Make sure you choose a treat that feels special and tastes delicious. Make this self-care time even more special by going outside, listening to music, or reading a book while you enjoy your chocolate or treat of choice.

Take Off Your Nail Polish

Living with chipped nail polish seems to be an expected part of being a mom, and some of us would rather have chipped polish than no polish at all. And while you may struggle sometimes to find the time (or money) for a mani and pedi (see Chapter 4), 5 minutes is time enough to take off the old polish, leaving you with clean nails, rather than nails that make you cringe when you look at them. You might even have enough time to file or quickly cut your nails, and then paint on a single coat of quick-dry polish (a coat of clear or shimmer polish is great).

Having nails that are cared for and look good can help boost your mood. If you like having your nails done, think of this 5-minute removal or polish change as holding you over between your longer nail-related self-care activities. Though this is practical self-care, because polish does need to come off at some point, it can also be emotional self-care, because we see our hands constantly. You may as well feel good about what you're seeing!

Sit Outside

The kids are fighting, someone is crying, you feel like you're constantly nagging people. Sometimes don't you just want to get out of your house? Thankfully there are many positive moments when you're a mom, but when you're feeling overwhelmed and especially *over it*, getting outside for 5 minutes can be a fantastic reset. A few minutes to sit still, connect with nature, and re-center can bring a more positive mood and outlook—and for some moms this time outside can be spiritual self-care too. While you're out there, add in other quick self-care activities as well. Repeat affirmations, stretch, or read, and feel free to extend the 5 minutes if you're able to.

If your kids are old enough, let them know you'll be right back, then step outside. If they're young, put them safely in their crib or play area, and bring your monitor outside with you. Depending on their age, you might put them in front of a favorite TV program or movie—if you have tweens or teens, they won't even notice you're gone! Sit outside, breathe in the fresh air, observe whatever is around you, and enjoy a cup of tea or coffee. Try adding this to your morning routine to start the day feeling focused and fresh. If you like, ask your kids to join you for this one. Simply invite them to sit (quietly) outside, help them notice what's around them, and encourage them to breathe deeply and enjoy the sensory experience.

Wash Your Face

Are you so tired at the end of your day that you do the bare minimum before you go to bed, skipping important tasks like washing your face? You're not alone. But washing your face is not only a practical task to remove dirt and makeup that can clog your pores; it's also a metaphor for cleaning off the day, so you can head to bed fresh-faced and with a clear mind.

Create a skincare routine that's easy to stick with—if you have too many steps, you may forgo it entirely—but commit to at least washing with cleanser and moisturizing. You can even have face cleansing wipes on hand (they're the adult version of baby wipes, meant to clean your face and remove makeup) for those times when you just don't have the energy to wash your face. Another way to make this a more consistent part of your day is to shift this 5-minute task to earlier in the evening rather than waiting until you're exhausted and ready to go to bed. For example, do it right after the kids have gone to bed. Or, if your kids are old enough, wash your face while they're doing their bedtime activities, like brushing teeth and putting on pajamas. Build this into your daily routine to help with consistency.

Try Freewriting

Having trouble organizing your thoughts or plans? Struggling to clear your mind? Give yourself some self-care in the form of freewriting. This practice is often used by writers before they start a project, and is writing for a set period of time without worrying about content, grammar, spelling, or even if your writing makes sense. This helps you clear out the ideas and thoughts that may be cluttering your mind, before you move on to your next task. Try this at any point in your day, but it may be particularly useful at the beginning or end of the day, especially if you tend to have a very active mind.

If you're struggling with how to start freewriting, grab a pen and paper or the notes feature on your phone, then try one or more of these activities: Write about your feelings, make lists of what you're thinking about, or take note of what you see, smell, and hear around you. Another option is to think of this writing activity as a mini journal and try using prompts like: "My highlight from yesterday was…"; "Something I'm struggling with is…"; "I felt like a good mom when…"; "I felt I could have done better when…"; etc. It's up to you if you want to keep your writing when you're done. It can be cathartic to toss the paper or delete the note on your phone. Go with whatever provides better mental and emotional self-care for you.

Pray

....

Taking the time to pray provides spiritual self-care, and the beauty of prayer is that it can be done anywhere, without needing anything extra to make it happen. Praying is often considered a religious practice, but who you pray to or what you pray about is up to you. Even if you're not religious, prayer gives you an opportunity to put your beliefs, thoughts, and wishes into the universe. Prayer can take place at home, to start or end your day, before a meal, or in an unexpected moment of silence, like before you head into the house once your kids have all left the car at the end of the day. Prayer can even be a family affair (like at mealtimes or before bed), and it can be done as many times in a day as you would like.

Even if you don't regularly pray, there can be emotional and mental benefits from giving it a try. You can pray silently, or you can speak out loud. Some people like to use a prayer journal to have a physical record of their prayers. Generally, prayer is a time to give thanks, express your hopes, and make requests. There is no right or wrong way to pray, so do what feels best for you. You might not need the full 5 minutes to pray, so consider starting and ending your prayer time with a minute of deep breathing, so that you begin and end your session feeling calm and grounded.

Experience Self-Massage

Let's face it—being a mom is stressful. And when you're stressed mentally, you often experience a physical reaction like muscle tension, which can cause additional negative effects like headaches, jaw pain, ongoing discomfort, and more. Stiff muscles are no joke. While a full-on massage to relieve those aches and pains would be nice, you don't always have the time and money for that, so self-massage can be a great option. (You can, of course, try to recruit a family member for this, but in case no one is willing, self-massage can be your backup plan.)

Depending on where you're experiencing muscle tension and pain, you'll need to adjust your technique for the massage. Google "self-massage for [where you experience tension]" for information from reliable sources like WebMD.com, or look for videos that show how to use your hands to apply pressure to different parts of the body. You can also invest in an item like a neck massager, or use something simple like a tennis ball to apply pressure to the part of your body where you're experiencing pain.

By relieving some of your muscle tension, you'll notice that you feel better. And by dealing with the physical manifestations of the stress, you'll experience less mental and emotional tension and will likely find yourself in a better mood as a result.

Make a Pitcher of Fruit Water

Staying hydrated is critical to your health and overall well-being. But if you're struggling to drink enough liquid, or plain water is feeling a bit mundane, try taking 5 minutes each evening to make a pitcher of flavored water for the next day. Simply fill a pitcher with water, add your favorite fruit: chopped or sliced, fresh or frozen (try the flavor combos mentioned here), let the water steep overnight, then drink throughout the day. You can also make this in the morning, but you generally want to give the fruit at least 2 hours in the water to create a good flavor.

Infused water can help curb sugar cravings, provide you with additional vitamins, and assist you with detoxing. Not only is this physical self-care, but the infused water is nice to look at, and can help to create a more positive mood throughout the day.

Treat yourself to a new combination each day, or rotate through several standard recipes. Recipes to try include: orange, lemon, and lime; strawberry and kiwi (lime optional); pineapple and coconut; strawberry, lemon, and basil; raspberry and mint; and blueberry and orange. Be creative and use what you have at home, or add a few ingredients to your shopping list each week specifically for your water.

Fill your water bottle with the prepared fruit water at the start of the day, and aim to finish drinking it by lunch. Refill your water bottle, and plan to drink the whole bottle by dinner, refilling it from your pitcher one more time to get you through the end of the day.

Complete a Leg or Ab Circuit

You might think that 5 minutes isn't enough to get in a good workout, but even if you only do leg work like squats and lunges, or do ab exercises for 5 minutes straight, you'll feel your muscles burn. Pick three or four exercises and rotate through sets of ten to fifteen reps until the time is up. For example, you can do squats, left-leg lunges, right-leg lunges, and then wide-leg squats, doing ten of each exercise for 5 minutes. Similarly, pick several variations of ab exercises, which can include crunches, planking, and leg lifts while lying down, and rotate through them.

If you're not confident in your ability to choose exercises, a quick online search will give you plenty of options. If necessary, refer to videos of the exercises you choose, so you do the exercises correctly. Consider adding these circuits into your daily routine, but alternate each body part to allow your muscles to rest. For example, complete the ab circuit on Monday, Wednesday, and Friday, and do the leg circuit on Tuesday, Thursday, and Saturday. As you get stronger, you can choose more difficult exercises, and/or challenge yourself to do more reps in 5 minutes, for some powerful physical self-care.

Note: if you have a newborn, be sure that your doctor has cleared you for exercise, and if it's been a while since you've worked out, be sure to listen to your body whenever you're active.

Do Nothing

How often do you sit still and do nothing? There may be many moments in your day when it *feels* like you do nothing—sitting in the car waiting for your kids, standing in the kitchen while the oven heats up, or waiting for a meeting to begin—but you probably don't look at those moments of nothing in a positive light. It may feel like you're wasting time. But time spent doing nothing intentionally is not wasted time; it is purposeful self-care.

Doing nothing is an act of mindfulness as you work to try to stay in the present moment, and at first, it might feel difficult, uncomfortable, or strange. You might find that your mind wanders to thoughts about what you have to do for the day or judgment about what you're doing (or not doing). Push that aside. Just sit, breathe, take in your surroundings, and don't *do* anything. Enjoy yourself and relax.

It can be helpful to do nothing in the moments when you feel most compelled to act. For example, when your kids are slow to gather all their belongings for school and your instinct is to jump in so you can get out of the house. Instead, do nothing. When the PTA is asking for volunteers and you know you're swamped, instead of chiming in, do nothing. Giving that space allows others to figure things out and gives you time to choose how you want to respond, rather than reacting quickly and regretting that reaction later. And, as a bonus, you're positively modeling for your children the act of being still and quiet, which is something that's easily lost in our fast-paced world.

Spend 5 Minutes Cleaning

As a mom, you know how tough it is to clean with kids around, but doing 5 minutes of this practical self-care will be worth it! By using 5 minutes at a time, you can keep your house tidier, and you know that makes a difference in your mood. Cleaning is one of those practical self-care activities that has a direct effect on how we think and feel, so it becomes mental and emotional self-care too. Obviously 5 minutes isn't going to make a *huge* difference, but 5 minutes of motivated, focused cleaning can make a *noticeable* difference in your house, especially if you do this activity regularly.

To get the most out of your 5 minutes, have a plan. For example, pick up all of the dirty laundry and put it in baskets, wipe down counters and tabletops in the kitchen, or pick up toys. Get your kids involved in this activity, too, especially if it's *their* things that need to be put away. And if you let everyone know that it's only for 5 minutes, you might hear fewer groans and arguments. Think about adding uplifting music to this task, cranking up the volume to get the whole house involved, and give this self-care activity a fun name like "fast 5 clean." You can easily build this self-care activity into your day. For example, clean for 5 minutes before you leave the house, 5 minutes when everyone is home, and then 5 minutes at the end of the day. Whether you work from home, stay home with your kids, or work outside the home, add in these moments regularly so that the state of your house doesn't get overwhelming. This can be adjusted to be a 15-minute activity if you prefer; just set a timer.

Open Your Windows

What is it about having kids at home that can turn a once fresh-smelling house into something that's, well, not quite as pleasant smelling? And if your kids are of a certain age (puberty!) and you have pets, sometimes your house may smell a bit…less than fresh. Sadly, you can become immune to it. Your nose and brain start to tune out those smells and you interpret them as neutral. Ick!

Take just 5 minutes to open the windows (if it's cold out, open them just a crack) to create a flow of fresh air in your home. Then use air freshener, light a scented candle or two (keep these away from your kids), diffuse essential oils, or use any other sort of room freshener to create a more pleasant smell within your home.

If you still have time after the windows are open and you've improved the scent in the house, then you can take out the trash or diaper bags, move the smelly laundry to the garage, or tackle any other items that are contributing to the scent of your home. These are practical steps that will likely boost your mood, as smells are often associated with memories (good and bad), so creating pleasant smells in your home is emotional self-care.

Create and Repeat Affirmations

Affirmations are strong, positive statements about you, written as if they are already true. For example, "I'm an awesome mom," or "I remain calm under stress." You may not always feel like an awesome mom, and you may not consistently handle stress as well as you'd like, but by creating these types of statements and repeating them often, you can change the way you think about yourself. Over time you'll begin to believe that you are an awesome mom, and not only will you *believe* that you can be calm under stress, but you'll likely begin to behave that way too.

The power of positive thought can't be overlooked, and affirmations are important mental self-care. Because they can also have a direct effect on your mood, affirmations are emotional self-care too. In just 5 minutes you can repeat your affirmations, create new ones to get you through your day, or strategically place your affirmations around your house and surroundings so that you see them throughout the day. Sticky notes are great for this, or set alarms on your phone labeled with your affirmations. Some moms are uncomfortable using affirmations at first, because they're *so* positive. If you are in this group, try them out and commit to sticking with them for a while. Repeat your affirmations regularly for maximum impact, and over time they'll be a part of your normal thinking habits—and your self-care routine.

Cuddle with Your Kids

Nothing beats the hugs, cuddles, and kisses from kids of any age. And physical touch, especially from your sweet kiddos, is so important for your emotional and mental self-care. If you have young kids, you're touched a lot, and it's normal to reach a point where you feel "touched out." Then, as your kids get older, they tend to interact less with physical touch. Regardless of the ages of your kids, cuddling and physical affection allow you to stay connected and likely fill you with positive emotions. Cuddle time might also create a space that allows your children to feel safe opening up to discuss things they're feeling and thinking. Then again, it may just be a nice time to be quiet (or silly) together. Five minutes may feel like a lot for some kids or even for you, so don't pressure your kids (or yourself!) to meet the 5-minute mark.

The purpose of physical touch—an extended hug, a brief snuggle, or even holding hands—is to meet your (and their) self-care needs. Invite your kids to sit with you. Depending on their ages and comfort levels this may mean having them sit on your lap, wrapping an arm around them, or holding hands. If your child has reached the tween/teen stage, and physical affection is not currently the norm, you might want to ask their permission. Simply cuddle, or read a book, talk about your day, reminisce, or even just watch TV. Starting this habit early can set the stage for a way to stay connected as your children get older. Tweens and teens may not want to be touched in public, but cuddles at home may feel just right.

Chapter 4
15-Minute Activities

As good as a 5-minute activity is, practicing self-care for 15 minutes starts to feel like you're really taking care of yourself. Like the 5-minute list, many of the self-care activities in this chapter are related to your emotional and mental self-care. Though it can sometimes feel like you're not in control of your mood or your thoughts, you can be, and self-care is critical to making that happen.

While 5-minute activities can be added into your schedule easily, you might find that it's a bit more difficult to make a 15-minute activity happen. But there's no reason why you can't have a 15-minute self-care activity happening every day if you plan for it. Take the time weekly or daily to plan at least one 15-minute self-care activity into your schedule. Whether you get up earlier, change up your usual routines, or simply put your kids in front of the TV for 15 minutes, you can make the time for this. Once you get into these activities, the time will go quickly, but you'll feel like you prioritized yourself *and* you'll be better off because of it.

Paint Your Nails

Let's face it, manicures are amazing, but for moms it can be hard to make them happen on a regular basis. And chances are, your nails get chipped or smudged once you get back to mom-life. However, having painted nails can make you feel more put together, and a pop of color can make you (and your kids) smile. Your nails don't have to be perfect, but you should take 10 minutes (leaving 5 to dry) to paint your nails in a color you love.

Add this into your weekly routine, and listen to music or watch a favorite TV show to make it even better. Consider when you can do this, so there's less chance of smudging or chipping, possibly after the kids go to bed. Buy a quick-drying top coat to set your nail polish instantly and they'll be dry to the touch in less than 5 minutes. That way, you can get back to what you need to do with pretty nails and some self-care under your belt.

This can be a great activity to include your kids in. Painting their nails along with yours (or letting them paint yours) can be a great way to practice self-care together. If young kids are doing the painting, be sure to have some cotton swabs and nail polish remover on hand!

Read a Chapter in a Book

When's the last time you read? Probably recently, but chances are it was a news story or blog post that you read quickly on your phone, or an email from work or school. Those don't count! Take the time to read something that you enjoy. Use any available time you have for this mental and emotional self-care, but if you love to read, aim to get in at least 15 minutes every few days. While each book will be different, 15 minutes usually allows enough time to get *into* a book. Try to find a natural stopping point, like the end of a chapter.

If you have school-age kids, read while they do homework. This sets a strong example of reading for fun, not just reading for school. You can also enjoy reading time as a family. Have everyone pick their own book (including picture books for the little ones), and set a timer for 15 minutes; no talking allowed. It will take time to get everyone in the habit of doing this, but it can be a worthwhile experience for the whole family, and it's an activity that can become part of your family's daily routine.

Keep a book in your car, too, or if you're reading an ebook, have it accessible on your phone. If you find yourself waiting yet again, use that time for self-care by reading. Remember, any type of book that brings you enjoyment is appropriate—no judgment over your choice!

Make a Healthy Smoothie

A smoothie is a snack that's healthy, helps fill you up, and gives you lots of essential nutrients. Once it's made, you can take it on the go, and there are plenty of recipes to try. This self-care can become a regular part of your routine without getting dull or feeling repetitive. Smoothies will generally include fruit (sometimes veggies), ice, yogurt, and possibly juice. You can also add protein powder to help you stay full longer. Fifteen minutes is the perfect amount of time to make the smoothie, including chopping ingredients, if needed, with time to clean up. Just throw all the ingredients in a blender (a baby food processor works, too, and is often the perfect size for a single-serve smoothie), blend the ingredients, rinse your blender, and then sit and enjoy. This self-care is practical and physical, as it gives you the nourishment you need, and if you take the time to sit and enjoy your smoothie, it's a mental and emotional self-care experience as well.

To make it easier to make a smoothie, keep sliced fruit in the freezer and skip the ice. Save time (and money) by cutting up your fruit before it gets overripe, and put it into a resealable bag in the freezer. This way you don't waste food and you're prepared anytime you want a smoothie. Add leafy greens, like kale or spinach, to your smoothie to give it an extra healthy kick. Try making a large batch so your kids can enjoy a smoothie too.

Use Social Media Purposefully

Platforms like *Facebook*, *Instagram*, and *Snapchat* make it easier to connect with friends and loved ones, and they can be fantastic tools to help you stay in touch when used with intention and purpose. But proceed with caution and keep track of the time so that the effects of your social media time are positive.

Set a timer for 15 minutes and log on with a plan in mind. For example, check the profiles of three people you haven't seen in a while to see what they're up to, and leave comments on their photos to connect. Or upload several new photos to an album so your family members can see what's going on with you. Choose to watch a video or two, or check a page or profile that helps you feel upbeat and happy (this is great for emotional self-care). Remember that it's easy to fall into the social media void, so when the timer goes off, log off. Learning to use social media with purpose will allow you to feel more connected with others, nurture relationships, and may also help you limit mindless checking, which typically takes away from our mental and emotional self-care.

Soak Your Feet

You're on your feet a lot. You're running kids from place to place, you're going to work, you're running errands, and you're moving around the house to get things done. Your feet are tired. Even if you don't notice it, they're tired. Take the time to soak your feet in an Epsom salt bath. Use a basic plastic basin or purchase a footbath that's just right for soaking. Or treat yourself and get one with bells and whistles, like Jacuzzi bubbles or textured rollers that help to massage your feet.

Regardless of what you use, the hot water just feels good, and adding Epsom salt can relieve pain, flush toxins from your body, and help to maintain magnesium levels. You can purchase Epsom salt inexpensively at the drug store, and can opt for a scented version to further enhance the self-care experience. Add about a half cup of Epsom salt to hot water, let it dissolve, and then sit with your feet in the tub, and relax as best you can. Clear your mind for some mental self-care along with this physical self-care. Or soak your feet while you do something else, like paying the bills or folding socks. When you're done soaking, paint your toenails or put on lotion with socks to help moisturize your feet for some extra self-care. This can also be a good activity to enjoy with your kids, depending on their ages and their willingness to sit still.

Journal

Remember when you were a kid and you wrote in your diary? You shared your fears, dreams, and the names of people you had a crush on? And then, when you were older, you may have started a journal but never stuck with it? Journals and journaling sometimes get a bad rap because there is often a start-and-stop nature to them. You might feel like you *should* journal and don't, turning journaling into a source of guilt.

But this isn't your mama's journaling. This is self-care! Journaling is one part reflection, one part committing words to paper. This second step is important, as it helps to focus your reflection efforts, gives you a written record of your thoughts and experiences, and can help you get the negative thoughts out of your head by putting them on paper.

Just take 15 minutes to write (you can start with this as a 5-minute activity if writing for 15 minutes sounds too overwhelming). What you write is up to you; keep it simple. Spelling, grammar, and handwriting don't count. You can even use bullet points. You might find it beneficial to write one or two sentences about what's positive in your life right now, one or two sentences about any struggles you're facing, and one or two sentences about what you're grateful for. The first and last points are super important because focusing on positivity and gratitude helps to create more optimistic thinking and emotions—which makes journaling emotional and mental self-care. And remember, journal as often as you feel like it. The frequency is up to you.

Enjoy Your Morning Coffee

How often have you made coffee or tea and then spilled, misplaced, or forgotten it? Sadly, for many moms, savoring a morning drink may be a thing of the past. For emotional and mental self-care, commit to sitting down to drink your coffee or tea (or juice) in a way that's enjoyable.

Make your beverage (take advantage of an automatic coffee maker if you can) and sit and enjoy it out of a beautiful mug or cup. If you don't have one you love, find one! Make this your morning cup, and let everyone know (nicely) that it's off-limits.

You may need to get up early to enjoy this drink while it's quiet, or let your family know that during a certain 15-minute window in the morning they're not to disturb you. If the family is already up, be sure to set things up so that everyone is taken care of. For example, set out things for their breakfast, let them know where the things they need can be found, and then sit and enjoy your coffee. If your kids are old enough and can respect your 15-minute experience, invite them to join you, with their own beverages and mugs of choice, so that you start the day off together with self-care.

Send a Card

Think back to the last time you received a handwritten note, like a thank-you note or a postcard. Chances are, it was a pleasant surprise that made you realize how much that person values you because they took the time to send it. Now's the time to do the same for someone else. Write a quick note to a friend or family member, letting them know you're thinking about them. It can be as simple as saying hello and wishing them well. If you know that they have an event coming up or challenge going on, send positive thoughts and encouragement their way.

This activity is emotional self-care for you (and likely for the recipient!), as well as a bit of social self-care. Even though you're not seeing the person, you're acknowledging and strengthening the connection you have with them. Think about keeping a pack of notecards with stamped envelopes and a pen in your bag. This way you can write quick notes when you find yourself with a bit of extra time, like waiting at doctors' appointments or when sports practice is running late. Just make sure you put the card in the mail! This is also a good activity to involve your kids in (though you might need more than 15 minutes), because everyone likes to receive mail.

Take an Intentional Shower

If you're a mom of a young child, you might not shower as often as you'd like; no judgment. Even as kids get older, you might find yourself rushing through your showers and not really enjoying them. A shower can be the ultimate self-care experience, but you need to go into it with intention...and probably a locked door.

To allow your shower to count as self-care, make sure you won't be interrupted, and take your time. You might even want to turn on music, light a candle, and turn down the lights. Make this time yours! Enjoy the feel of the water as it hits your body, close your eyes, and breathe deeply, aiming to clear your mind for some mental self-care. You should also use products that feel and smell great. Instead of rushing through washing your hair and body, massage your scalp, inhale the scents, and enjoy the positive emotions that will likely occur.

Use your fluffiest towel to dry off and, if you have time, use a silky, scented lotion on your body before you get dressed and return to your day. This intentional shower can be great at the end of your day to wind down for bed, but it can also happen any time you have 15 minutes and can handle having wet hair. Or use a shower cap and focus on your body!

Do Core Work

Having a strong core is critical for everyone, but especially for moms. Think about all the moving, lifting, and carrying that you do. Yes, your core includes your abdominal muscles, but it also includes your back muscles and your pelvic floor. (A strong core can also help with incontinence. Thanks, kids, for that pregnancy souvenir!) When you have a strong core, you'll be less likely to experience back pain, you'll feel stronger, and your clothes might fit better too! This physical self-care shouldn't be overlooked.

To improve your core strength, try a circuit of the following exercises, being mindful that the movements are controlled, you're aware of your breathing while you do these exercises, and you pay attention to how your body is feeling. Core exercise can include crunches, but also planks (hold a push-up position), bridges (lie down, feet on the floor with your knees bent, then lift your hips), and super (wo)man exercises (lie flat on your stomach, arms extended, and raise your arms and feet). Search for a variety of these core exercises online, as well as Pilates workouts, which also help strengthen your core. Be sure to find images and videos of the exercises, so you use proper form. If you currently have a weak core (which many moms do), you may need to work up to 15 minutes.

Get Dressed in an Outfit You Love

What you wear and how you feel in your clothes have a direct influence on how you feel about yourself. Some moms get into a routine, wearing the same types of clothes over and over or the same articles of clothing again and again. While this predictability can help to simplify your busy life, it's also important to choose items of clothing that you feel good in. After all, when you're thinking and feeling positively, you're more likely to have the type of day you want to have.

You might find that the clothes you once loved don't fit the way they used to, or that your favorite garments have seen better days. Is that a paint stain on your favorite shirt? Does glitter glue come off shoes? What about that spaghetti sauce on those pants you love; can you save them? Sadly, wear and tear on clothes is a normal consequence of being a mom, though it does get better as the kids get older. Once in a while, take the time to step out of your usual clothes and get dressed in an outfit you feel good in, for some mental and emotional self-care. It doesn't matter if it's a bit dressy for the occasion or feels out of the norm for you; make sure you love what you're wearing. And if you're at a stage of life where this is a struggle and you find that you're taking things on and off, perhaps set aside more time for a closet decluttering session and find all the clothes you feel good in *now*. See "Organize Your Closet" in Chapter 7 for some ideas!

Listen to *Your* Music in the Car

When's the last time you listened to music that you wanted to while you were in the car? It's probably been a while. Whether you're constantly listening to a movie soundtrack on repeat or a kid's *Pandora* station, you're singing songs your kids like, or you're cringing over what your tween or teen is listening to, *your* music probably feels like a thing of the past. It's time to change that, because music can boost your mood, and for many moms it's an instant pick-me-up.

Let your kids know that you'll be playing *your* music for 15 minutes, and when the time is up, you'll put their music back on. Choose music that you love but that's also kid-appropriate, and enjoy! Want to dance while you drive? Go for it, but do it safely. If the kids complain, tell them the 15-minute timer starts over. Get your self-care in! In addition to this mental and emotional self-care for you, you're also showing your kids that your interests matter and are just as important as theirs. This is an essential lesson for you *and* for them. It's important that they learn that everyone's preferences have value and are worth making time for. Over time you'll likely find music you can compromise on, and get more than 15 minutes of your music at a time.

Figure Out Your Triggers
and How to Deal

We all have triggers as moms—those things that make us blow up and react in ways we're not proud of. Having your buttons pushed is not a fun experience for anyone (though our kids do sometimes seem to find joy in it!), and the way we react in those situations is typically upsetting for everyone involved. Maybe you get upset because your kid spilled a sticky drink at an inconvenient time. Or maybe your kids just aren't listening to you, and you have a big reaction when you have to say things more than once or twice. Sometimes our triggers aren't situation specific, but rather happen when we're hungry or overtired.

In this self-care activity, take 15 minutes (on more than one occasion, if needed) to figure out what your triggers are and work to change how you react to those triggers. Start by writing down your triggers and then plan for how to deal with them. For example, if your trigger is spilled drinks, then you plan that in addition to using more cups with lids, if a drink gets spilled, you'll take a breath, walk out of the room, and come back a minute later when you can deal with it calmly. If your trigger is more general, like you blow up when you're tired or hungry, find ways to get more sleep, and set reminders on your phone to make sure you take the time to eat. You'll be less snappy with your kids, and you'll all be happier. The goal is to plan for how to respond, rather than simply reacting with strong, negative emotions. This is practical self-care, but the change in your reactions will be mental and emotional self-care as well.

Get Up 15 Minutes Early

Mornings can be chaotic when you have kids, even if you're organized and have routines in place. Once everyone is up, especially on weekdays, it's usually about checking things off the list so you can get out the door. Instead of starting your day with everyone else, consider getting a head start. Waking up even 15 minutes before your family can make a huge difference in how the morning activities go, and that can influence the rest of your day. (That said, if you have a kid who is a super-early riser and keeps busy in the morning, you don't need to get up 15 minutes before *that* kid; get up 15 minutes before the day really starts at your house.)

Use your extra 15 minutes in whatever way is best for you. Do a self-care activity with this time: sit in silence, do some breathing exercises, or pray, and start your day feeling grounded. Another option is to check a practical task off your list, like balancing your checkbook or getting things situated around the house so that the morning flows better. Basically, your goal is to start your day off in the way you want, rather than being influenced by the amped-up (sometimes moody) energy that can happen once kids are awake and everyone is trying to get out of the house.

Do a Face or Hair Mask

Taking some time to use a face or hair mask (or both!) helps to hydrate, cleanse, and refresh your hair and skin, and is a nice way to prioritize yourself without having to leave the house. Beauty treatments are emotional and practical self-care and a fun treat!

You can purchase a variety of masks at your local pharmacy or big box store, or online through your favorite retailer. Face and hair masks don't need to be expensive, but splurge if you want to. You can also make your own masks at home by searching for recipes online. Chances are you have ingredients already in your house that you can use.

A mask can also be a fun activity to do with your kids, especially teens who also want some pampering. Consider inviting them to join you for this self-care. And once you apply your face or hair mask, try to sit and do additional self-care activities while you let the mask do its work. Check off practical self-care by meal planning or cleaning up a room, add in mental self-care by reading, or do some spiritual self-care with prayer. There are plenty of options when you layer your self-care!

Check Something Off Your To-Do List

Your daily to-do list is probably a mile long. Between kids, home, work, and personal chores, it may feel like nothing gets checked off your list, or even that more tasks are added as the day progresses. Make it a point to give yourself some self-care and use your 15 minutes to check something off your list! Whether you keep track of what you need to get done on a pad of paper, an app, or even a mental list, it just feels good when you can check something off. Decide on one item that you can complete and then get it done! This is practical self-care, but the task that you complete may have additional self-care benefits. For example, you can call in that prescription refill you've been meaning to get to, or do the ab circuit that's supposed to happen daily. Both are physical self-care. Send those emails you've been meaning to get out, which is also mental self-care, because once they're sent, you can stop thinking about them. You get the idea.

With 15 minutes you might be able to check several small to-dos off your list, or tackle one bigger task, but definitely pick one item that you can complete. This isn't an activity to chip away at. Accomplishing just about anything on your list will make you feel good about getting something *done.*

Make a List of Your Friends to Stay in Touch With

Pre-kids, making a list of your friends might have seemed like a silly idea. You didn't need a list! You knew who the important people were and you stayed in touch. For a mom, things can be different. It can be hard to find time to see and connect with people, and simply *remembering* to reach out to certain people can be difficult. You may find that you don't see friends who only live a few miles away because their kids are in different schools, or you have kids of different ages and don't run in the same circles. Life moves so quickly, and everyone is busy, so it's very easy to lose track of each other.

To combat this, go through your phone and email and create a list of the people you really want to keep in touch with and plan get-togethers with. Then keep this list in your phone or your wallet. When you have 5 minutes, you can refer to this list and send texts to say hello or start planning a playdate or an adult date. With 15 minutes, you can give these people a call to check in. And when you have more time, you can plan meet-ups, playdates, dinners, and more. This is a practical step to ensure that you continue social self-care with the people who matter to you. They're worth it—and so are you.

Color

A few years back, coloring became *the* thing for adults to help them relax and quiet their minds. Though the craze may have hit its peak, this activity is more than just a passing trend. It may not seem like it, but sitting down to color can be mental and emotional self-care. As you color, you may find a feeling of peace come over you. Some moms find that if they're feeling anxious, purposeful coloring can help dissipate the negative feelings. This self-care activity also allows you to be creative, possibly fueling your soul as well.

As a mom, you may have coloring books and crayons, markers, and colored pencils throughout your house, and while you can use these, you may want to invest in your own coloring supplies. Because coloring became such a trend, there are coloring books for adults in many styles and themes, from geographic designs and whimsical nature images to curse words in the form of art. There's sure to be something that appeals to you and your adult sense of style. You can also find printable coloring pages online so that you don't have to wait to get your hands on a book.

Coloring can be done with your kids, or it can be an activity that you do near them when you need to be present but not completely focused on them, such as when they're doing homework and you need to be available for the occasional question. Coloring can replace the mindless scrolling on your phone, and can help you clear your mind and zone out in a good way.

Have a Dance Party

As you know, music can be a great mood booster and stress reliever. When you add dance to it, you add physical self-care to the mix! This physical self-care adds up to help you meet your weekly exercise goals, and will likely feel like mental and emotional self-care too. When you're lost in dance, your mind won't be focused on anything else, and it's hard to be in a bad mood after a dance party because of the endorphins your body releases when you move. Now, while dancing *should* be a fun experience, your judgment about your perceived dance skills might get in the way. Kick that doubt to the curb; everyone can dance. The only rules are to move your body and have fun.

Dance parties can happen on your own, but are also really fun when your kids join in. Pick music you'll all enjoy, or introduce them to your favorite music, and just move! You can encourage them to teach you a dance move, shadow each other and mirror each other's moves, or just move however you're inspired to. Having a dance party is a great way to shift the mood in the house when things are tense or dreary, or you just need to get going for something. These at-home dance parties will also help give you and your kids the confidence to dance in front of others, which is a great life skill to have. And while dancing for 15 minutes is great, you can dance for any amount of time and really reap the self-care benefits.

Create a Bedtime Routine

The end of the day can be a bit stressful, which runs counter to what you're trying to do: wind down and go to sleep. In order to calm down and relax, try creating—and following through with—a bedtime routine as a form of self-care. Before you create your routine, think about what usually happens at the end of your day and how you're feeling when you try to go to bed. Also think about how long it typically takes you to fall asleep. All of this will influence what you want to do with your time right before bed.

When creating your routine, include self-care activities that are practical in nature, like washing up and brushing your teeth, but also include mental and emotional self-care activities to help put you in a relaxed frame of mind and a positive mood before bed. Your routine can include some of the 5-minute activities from Chapter 3, like applying lotion, or one or two 15-minute activities from this chapter, such as meditating, reading, listening to soft music or a guided meditation, or journaling (this one is great if you tend to have an active mind at bedtime). Your bedtime routine can extend beyond 15 minutes, if needed, and should probably include powering down your electronics and turning off the TV, especially if your mind continues to be active once your head hits the pillow. Feel free to change up what you do, but be consistent with the activities that most help you get into bedtime mode.

Do Your Full Makeup

In the "Create (and Use!) a 5-Minute Makeup Routine" in Chapter 3, you learned how to enhance your beauty in 5 minutes, and that's great! But with self-care, more is always better, so give yourself another 10 minutes when you can to build on that routine and leave the house feeling great!

Applying makeup can be a very personal experience and may be mental and emotional self-care for you. Do your makeup in a way that makes you feel your best, and feel free to change up your daily routine as much as you'd like. Makeup is something you can have fun with!

Some moms will want more than 15 minutes to really do their makeup, so if that's you, plan the extended time into your schedule when you can, but consider having a quicker go-to routine that's about 15 minutes for your typical day and then a longer routine for when you have the time. And if you don't need the full 15 minutes, it can be useful to plan this into your schedule and then you can use the extra time for some additional self-care like deep breathing, affirmations, or prayer.

Meditate

Meditation is the practice of training yourself to be still and more in the moment. When you meditate, the idea is to notice your thoughts and observe them without judgment. Mindfulness, which we discussed in "Practice Mindfulness" in Chapter 3, is being present; meditation is the practice of being mindful. Meditation practice is best when it's done regularly, so consider finding a consistent time in your daily routine when you can add in 15 minutes of meditation.

Find a place where you can sit comfortably and aren't likely to be interrupted. Focus on your breathing, refocusing on it when your mind wanders. You'll notice things about your body and your surroundings. Don't judge yourself or your thoughts. Some people use a mantra to help with meditation (for example, the sound "om"), but this may keep you from focusing on your breathing.

Meditation may have an immediate effect, leaving you feeling calm and more mentally clear, which is fantastic emotional and mental self-care. But the real gift of meditation is the effect it has in the big picture. Ongoing meditation practice allows you to be more mindful in day-to-day life, which can help you feel more grounded and in control. It can help you choose how to respond, as opposed to randomly reacting to those many challenging moments that are thrown at you as a mom. Meditating with your kids is a great way for everyone to get self-care, can help increase your kids' ability to be mindful, and as a result can improve everyone's relationships and interactions.

Get Clear on Your Boundaries

Because you're a mom, people may often ask for your help, time, or involvement, and sometimes they automatically assume you'll say yes. It's easy to get burned out when you're constantly doing things for other people, which means you need to set some boundaries. Setting and maintaining boundaries and saying no to things you don't really want to do allows you to say yes to what's important to you. This is practical self-care that will ultimately become mental and emotional self-care.

Take 15 minutes to get clear on the boundaries you need to set for yourself. For example, no more birthday parties next month, only volunteer for what you're excited about, and no more accepting invitations to events you don't want to go to. Then, once you're clear on what your boundaries are, brainstorm three to five ways you can nicely decline those requests. Try something like, "Thank you for asking me, but unfortunately I don't have time right now to devote to that," or "I appreciate that you'd like me to be involved, but I'm maxed out right now." If those feel too direct for your comfort level, try something like, "I need to check my schedule before I commit to that." That way you can stall in person, then send an email later to decline or be clear on how you can be involved. Practice saying these things out loud and picture yourself saying them to others. The more you do this, the better you'll get at it. Remember, people can be pushy and continue to ask even after you've declined, so be willing to stand your ground. Be aware that setting and sticking to boundaries can be uncomfortable at first, but it will be worth it for you and your family.

Read a Spiritual Book

Spiritual self-care may mean something different to everyone, so it's important for you to figure out how you can feed your spirit. For many moms, reading is a strong way to get spiritual self-care. Allow yourself 15 minutes for reading passages in the Bible, another book that deepens your understanding of religion or spirituality, or any book that feeds your soul. Then reflect on what you read to deepen the spiritual self-care.

While no one likes to have their reading time interrupted, it might be even more important that your spiritual reading time is uninterrupted since spiritual practices tend to be deeply meaningful and profound. Consider when and where you can get the space to focus on your reading. You may find that the best time is at the start of the day, before the rest of the members of your family are awake, or at the close of your day so you can head to bed with a nourished soul. The frequency of this activity is up to you, so consider your personal spiritual needs. You can also make this family time, reading aloud, or each reading silently but together. However, if your kids are at a stage where they complain about this, even if it's important to you that they are exposed to religious or spiritual reading, consider prioritizing your own needs from time to time and do this reading on your own.

Create a Plan for Your Laundry

Laundry is one of those tasks that is often difficult to control. Practice practical self-care by taking 15 minutes to think more strategically about your laundry challenges and come up with a plan that will help you conquer the laundry mountain.

For example, if you currently try to do laundry all in one day, and then can't complete the task, try doing just one load a day, getting in the habit of putting a load into the washer when you walk in the door after work, drying it that night, and folding as you watch TV after the kids' bedtime. If you always forget that there is a load in the washing machine, making you redo load after load, get in the habit of setting alarms to remind you. Or your plan for the laundry might include delegating certain steps to family members, like making sure your younger kids collect all the dirty laundry in one place, so you're not using time to track it all down, or requiring that your older kids help you fold and put away. Even your toddler can help match socks!

Also, consider ways to simplify this task. For example, do you need to sort all the socks into pairs, or can your child match them themselves as they pull them from the basket or drawer when they get dressed? Does underwear need to be folded? Consider all the ways you can organize laundry more efficiently, with support from your family members, so that you have fewer times when the laundry (both dirty and clean) takes over your home.

Play a Brain Game on Your Phone

Technology is all around us. Sometimes it can get a bit out of hand, like when you spend too much time on social media or are constantly plugged in. But being on your phone, even when your kids are around, doesn't have to be a source of guilt! Be purposeful about how and when you use your phone, and instead of mindless scrolling or checking, use it for some mental stimulation and self-care.

There are many free apps and games that will work your brain. Love classic sudoku? There's an app for that. Is mah-jongg more your style? There's an app for that too! From traditional puzzles to Tetris-style video games, there are tons of ways to give your brain a workout, which is important to keep you sharp and mentally fit (and to try to combat "baby brain," which seems to last well beyond the baby stage!). Playing games on your phone *can* become a big time-suck, so set a timer for 15 minutes and move on when the timer goes off. Challenge yourself by setting goals and trying new games, in addition to playing your favorites. Ask your kids for suggestions and introduce them to your favorite games, playing with them or against them for some fun family bonding and mental self-care for everyone.

Start a Group Text and Plan a Night Out

Spending time with your friends is a great way to experience social self-care, and while you probably can't plan a night out with friends in 15 minutes, you *can* start the ball rolling. So get out your phone and your calendar and send a group text to your friends. In the first text, it's helpful to not only mention that you'd like to get together, but to give some idea about the timing, and even details about the type of get-together. For example, let them know you think it would be fun to go to happy hour one weeknight next month. That way, people can start looking at specifics in their calendars. Say something like, "Let us know the dates that work for you as soon as possible, so we can firm it up and get it on the calendar." You can even use an online calendar tool like Doodle or LettuceMeet to help you see everyone's availability.

While a night out with your partner and other couples or a get-together with a group of your friends are both strong self-care choices, choosing to go with just *your* friends, especially if they're parents, may be easier. If one half of the couple is going out, then ideally the partners can be home with the kids. If your partner has negative feelings about this, remind them about *their* self-care and encourage them to plan a night out with their friends, when you'll be home with the kids. This way, you each get important time away with friends.

Eat Something

Being *hangry* is a real thing (that's being both hungry and angry, if you haven't heard the term). Eating is practical self-care that goes a long way toward making sure you can take care of your other self-care needs and the daily tasks you're responsible for. When your blood sugar or glucose level drops, your brain can't function at its best, you're more likely to be irritable, and things can go haywire quickly. As a mom, you may tend to forget to eat, or you may not eat enough. When you're taking care of everyone else, running from one thing to the next, or powering through your workday (or possibly *all* of those), sometimes it can be hard to take good care of yourself.

Set your alarm if you need help remembering, and take 15 minutes to stop what you're doing and eat. This may require some planning, so be sure to have quick and healthy food options available to you. For example, if you're going to be out of the house, get in the habit of stocking your purse or car with snacks like nuts, granola bars, fruit, and water. Think ahead for your day and determine if you'll be out at mealtime. If so, it might make sense to bring a lunch with you so that you can be sure to eat. Remember that you can't function at your best without fuel, which means you're less likely to do a good job at whatever you are doing, and chances are you won't feel your best if you skip meals or are low on calories.

Cultivate Positive Thinking

Even for the most positive of moms, negative thoughts are common. Yes, it's normal to have negative thoughts about yourself, your children, and your ability to "do it all" well. It's normal to question yourself, compare yourself to others, and put yourself down. But the reality is that it isn't healthy and it makes you feel bad. The good news? It *can* be changed.

There is a simple formula you can use to change your negative thinking: stop, drop, and roll. When you notice a negative thought, like "Why am I failing at this today?" tell yourself to *Stop*! Internally, let yourself know that this way of thinking isn't okay. Then drop some words of kindness, positivity, and/or logic on yourself, saying things like "I'm doing better than I give myself credit for" or "I showed up; that's what's important." Then roll into your next activity in a more positive frame of mind.

Take 15 minutes to write down some of the negative or distracting thoughts you tend to have, then write down what you can say to yourself instead. Preparing positive words that you can drop on yourself when you veer into negativity makes it easier to actually do it in the moment. Keep in mind that even if you don't feel different right away, positive thinking and using stop, drop, and roll are important mental self-care that will create more positive emotions over time. That said, if you struggle with deep, dark, ongoing negative thinking, don't be afraid to reach out for support. Doctors' visits and therapy sessions are important self-care too.

Chapter 5

30-Minute Activities

When you commit to setting aside 30 minutes at a time for self-care, the doors open to the types of activities you can do. Social self-care becomes more realistic, you can give yourself time to get out of the house (even if it's brief), and you can tackle practical self-care tasks that take more time, like working on your budget or meal planning. Thirty-minute activities may also allow you to touch on more types of self-care within one activity. Yes, those shorter self-care habits and activities are important, but they shouldn't be all you do to take care of yourself.

For some moms, it may feel like *too much* to set aside 30 minutes, or you may try but then get interrupted. Make 30 minutes the goal to start, even if you don't reach the full time. The more you practice longer stretches of self-care, the better you'll get at it, and the more understanding the people around you will be about the importance of that time. To give yourself the best chance of having these longer periods of time, proactively schedule them into your week and get the support you need to make them happen.

Declutter

For many moms, clutter is the bane of their existence: house clutter, school clutter, mental clutter...there's just too much stuff! Take 30 minutes and try to tackle that one area of your home that makes you cringe when you look at it. Maybe it's the spot where all the school-work accumulates, or the place where backpacks, shoes, sports equipment, and all the other *things* end up. Thirty minutes may not be enough to tackle the whole area, but it's typically enough time to make a noticeable dent.

Start by tossing anything broken or unusable, recycle (or shred) the paper that's not needed, and put anything that can be given away or sold in a bag. Then, when you're left with only what *should* be in that space, work on organizing it in a way that makes sense, creating a spot for everything. If there's not enough room, you may feel that you need more space or need to buy items to help you reorganize. While these things may be true, consider if you can remove anything else from the area first. Then, once you've pared down to only the essentials and have the space well organized, you'll have a much easier time keeping the clutter away. Now when you look at this space, you'll feel much better. If this is an area that your whole family uses, be sure to make it clear to them what's allowed there and where things go so everyone can be involved in keeping this space clutter-free and organized.

Go Outside for a Walk

Getting outside is self-care on its own. The change of scenery, the beauty of nature, and the way you can get out of your head and be more present are all important for mental, emotional, and, for some, spiritual self-care. By walking, you're adding in physical self-care. If there are others who can walk with you, this activity can also give you social self-care. But with only 30 minutes, you may not always be able to have someone join you. That's okay! Doing this with someone else isn't a must; the focus is more on you getting out, into nature, and getting some physical activity. In the colder months consider an offbeat location, like the mall or a warehouse store, to get in a stroll.

If you're a new mom or have young kids, daily walks can be a fantastic and important part of your routine. New babies will often enjoy riding in a stroller or carrier, and toddlers will be happy checking out the scenery, especially if you include snacks or their favorite toy in the stroller. Depending on the ages and temperaments of your older kids, you might invite them to join you on the walk, but remember that this is meant to be self-care for you. If you think they'll disrupt *your* self-care, it may be best for your walk to be kid-free.

Watch a Sitcom or Reality TV

Struggling to figure out how to decompress during your 30 minutes of self-care? Try watching something enjoyable on TV! Sitcoms are a great choice because most are over in half an hour, and many moms love to watch reality TV as a guilty pleasure. For this self-care activity, drop the guilt and enjoy watching the lives of others in bite-sized, 30-minute chunks. Keep in mind that for this activity, not all TV shows are created equal. Sitcoms are (generally) positive and light in nature, as are many reality shows, but while you may like to watch dramas and horror shows at other times, for self-care choose something that will lead to more positive thoughts and emotions.

Been a while since you've enjoyed a show and not sure what to watch? Ask some of your friends or coworkers what they're watching. This will give you a great way to connect with each other, like sending texts about who received the rose on *The Bachelor*, or chatting at work about the latest happenings on the show they introduced you to. You can also revisit a favorite show, like *Friends*, *The Office*, or *How I Met Your Mother* on *Netflix*, or On Demand. If you have a DVR, record a few options so you'll be ready for this emotional self-care activity whenever you need it.

Plan for a Vacation

In Chapter 8 we will talk about self-care goals. Several of these extended activities involve travel, which means they don't happen spontaneously, because as a parent, spontaneous travel *without kids* is extremely unlikely. A vacation, or even a night away, requires planning, researching, coordinating, and more. Not only do you need to plan the details of where you're going and how you're getting there, but you also need someone (or several people) to take care of your kids (or keep an eye on your teens) while you're away. So take some time and start to plan that trip!

While you might not get a full trip planned in half an hour, it may not happen at all if you don't make the time to get organized. When you have a trip in mind, you might find yourself searching travel deal sites while you should be folding laundry, looking at hotel options while you're at the park with your kids, or daydreaming about getting away. While all of this is enjoyable, it's not concrete action geared toward making the trip happen. Yes, you can still search at other times, but this practical self-care is about making plans and getting things organized so that your trip can happen and you can leave feeling good.

Depending on the trip and amount of time away, you might spend your 30 minutes researching and booking a hotel, arranging flights, securing reservations for things like meals or excursions, contacting potential sitters, and organizing information about kids' schedules and needs for those sitters. When the trip gets closer, use this 30-minute self-care time to pack and organize the house for your time away. Depending on the length and destination of your trip, add several of these 30-minute planning sessions into each month to help you get ready and feel good about taking some time away.

Meal Plan for the Week

Why do moms have to be responsible for so many meals for so many people? It may be one of our biggest challenges! And, without fail, we all have moments when we have no idea what to make, or we had a plan, only to find we're missing a key ingredient (or two!). Fortunately, spending 30 minutes meal planning can help you get the challenges of mealtime under control. There are many ways to meal plan, but essentially, you just need to make the time to decide what you'll serve at mealtime for a certain period of time, possibly for the week, but maybe for just a few days to get started.

Consider breakfast, lunch, and dinner. What will your family eat? Once that's determined, create a shopping list, being sure to take a look at what you already have on hand before you shop. For busy families with lots of after-school and evening activities happening, take this into account in your planning. You may have a meal for the family that keeps well as leftovers for the people who come home late. You can also do double batches of dishes to have for lunches the next day or dinner later in the week. Remember, meals can be simple and you don't have to be a great cook (or even like cooking!). The idea is that you're taking the guesswork out of the day-to-day by planning. Over time meal planning will take less and less time. As you go, save even more time by keeping track of the meals that work well for your family (and you), and continue to use those as part of your plan going forward.

Get a Library Card

Having a library card is one of the best ways to access free and low-cost self-care. Signing up for a library card is easy (typically you just have to bring proof of your address to your local branch). Once you have your card, you can check out books, magazines, and DVDs, and download audio and ebooks. Some libraries even offer enrichment classes, workshops, and more, which are typically free or have a minimal cost to join. An additional perk of some library systems is the ability to gain entry to local museums and activities for reduced or free admission. Take the time to get a library card and research the membership perks. It is well worth it.

When you check out books from the library (hard copy, ebook, or audiobook), you're able to give yourself mental and emotional self-care by giving yourself mental stimulation and experiencing positive emotions from what you read. You can read or listen during any available time you have, and audiobooks can be listened to while you complete household chores, making these activities feel less chore-like. You don't need to have a library card to go to the library, and visiting the library can also be a peaceful experience, and one your kids can participate in with you, making this 30 minutes of self-care well spent.

Work On a Puzzle

Find a place in your house where you (and possibly your family) can do a puzzle. Choose a spot where it won't be disturbed so that you can keep the puzzle out until you finish it. If you haven't done puzzles before, they may challenge you mentally (which is positive for mental self-care) and sometimes cause frustration, but overall, they tend to foster positive emotions as you, piece by piece, build and then complete a puzzle. This self-care activity can also be a positive social experience for you and your family, as it helps everyone get away from technology and screens for a while. You can certainly work on a puzzle for less time (maybe you fill 5 minutes looking for a few pieces to fill in), but 30 minutes allows you to get focused on and immersed in the task.

Puzzles can be fun tasks for families to work on, and having an in-progress puzzle readily available allows for spontaneous work on the puzzle as well as self-care. There are many different kinds of puzzles, with different styles, numbers of pieces, and sizes of pieces, so if you and your children won't enjoy the same type or you have several age groups in your household, consider having two (or more) puzzles going at the same time. If you really enjoy doing puzzles, it can become an expensive habit. Consider finding another family or two to trade puzzles with, but be sure to set guidelines that all pieces must be accounted for. (Though you can often find puzzles at garage sales and thrift stores, there is no guarantee that all of the pieces will be there.)

Give Yourself a Facial

Doing an at-home facial can be a fun way to indulge. Set up your space to encourage maximum relaxation and enjoyment. Light scented candles or diffuse essential oils, turn on some music you enjoy, and close the door (lock it if you need to!). First, wash your face, removing any dirt and makeup. You can use an exfoliating facial cleanser or use a face wash for your skin type and exfoliate after (be gentle with your skin!). Then steam your face to help open up your pores. Boil water or fill a sink with very hot water, place a towel over your head and shoulders, and lean your face (carefully!) over the water, making sure the steam feels warm on your face, not hot. Feel free to add rose petals, essential oils, or an herb, such as rosemary, to the water for a lovely scent while you steam.

Next, do a facial mask, homemade (try $\frac{1}{4}$ cup plain yogurt, 2 tablespoons honey, and a ripe banana mixed together) or store-bought, and then give your skin another treat by misting on a toner once your mask has been washed off. Add an anti-aging or nutrient serum if you like. Last, you're ready to moisturize! Take your time on this final step, and gently massage your face as you apply the moisturizer. If you'd like, invite your kids or your friends to join you for this indulgent self-care experience!

Get Lost in a Book

As you learned in the "Read a Chapter in a Book" activity in Chapter 4, 15 minutes of reading is nice, but 30 minutes is even better! With half an hour you can get more absorbed in whatever you're reading, quiet your mind, and enjoy how this self-care experience engages your mind and your emotions. Though reading Internet articles can also be self-care, consider spending this time reading a book or even a magazine, so you engage with in-depth content and take a break from screens.

It's great to include your school-age kids in a 30-minute self-care reading session. Chances are, they already have daily reading assignments and you can spend your time reading together. Depending on the ages of your kids, and your shared interests, you may be able to find books to read together, like the Harry Potter series, Lord of the Rings, or the latest bestseller. You can each read on your own and then discuss what you've read (like a mini book club), or read aloud to your child. Either way, you're also getting social self-care when you get others involved in the activity. If you'd rather read by yourself, that's fine too. Read when the kids aren't around, maybe at the start or end of the day. If you tend to mindlessly watch TV when the day is done, read a book for a half hour instead, or close out your day reading to help you wind down for bed, possibly adding it to your bedtime routine.

Clean for 30 Minutes

Cleaning is a chore. It just is. But it is also critical practical self-care. When your house is dirty, you don't feel your best. We all have different tolerance levels for messes and dirt, but as a mom, you may feel that your living space likely is not as neat or as clean as you'd like. With 5 minutes of cleaning, mentioned in Chapter 3, you can keep some of the chaos away, but let's face it, you likely need more time than that to *really* clean.

Fortunately, if you go about cleaning intentionally and with energy, you can be very productive in just 30 minutes. Think about building 30 minutes into your schedule several times a week to help keep up with the cleaning, which will then cut back on the time you spend cleaning on your days off (which is when most of us try to tackle these types of chores!). So set a timer for 30 minutes and clean! Focus on one area, putting things back where they belong, and then tackle the dirt. In an ideal world, your kids will be involved too. Delegate chores or tasks to them, and you can be even more productive with your 30 minutes. For example, have the kids put items away and you take care of dirt removal. If you're dealing with lots of complaints, consider starting with a shorter time frame for your kids and have them work up to 30 minutes. You can also incentivize the task. Tell them that if they clean for 30 minutes twice a week without complaint, you'll make a special meal or they can choose the menu. Remember, you didn't make all of the mess—you shouldn't have to clean it all!

Work Out

The Centers for Disease Control and Prevention (CDC) recommend that adults do at least 150 minutes of moderate-intensity aerobic activity each week. If you do the math, that works out to five 30-minute sessions each week. Some weeks you'll go over this, other weeks you won't, but keep in mind that it's important to prioritize physical self-care to help maintain both physical and mental health. Many moms think and feel better when they exercise regularly. And the CDC also confirms that something is better than nothing when it comes to activity and exercise, so do your best to fit this self-care activity into your routine! With 30 minutes you can go for a brisk walk (or jog if you're ready for it), find an exercise routine online, or simply turn on some high-energy music and dance.

You can include your kids in your workout. Invite them to participate, or have them help you out. If you have a baby or young toddler, they can act as a weight for your exercises. Hold or wear them while you squat and lunge (make sure you're physically ready for that). By working out in front of your kids, you set a positive example about exercise.

Keep in mind that your workout may be derailed here and there. For instance, young kids may see planking as an invitation to climb on top of you or under you. But the great thing about doing your workout while your kids are around is that you get to do your self-care while staying engaged with them. Over time everyone will get into a routine and your 30-minute workouts will become more productive.

Engage in Spiritual Practice

Using 30 minutes of your time to devote to your spiritual self-care will feed your soul and likely provide mental and emotional self-care as well. It's up to you to determine what sort of spiritual activities meet your needs, and how often you want to fit them into your schedule, but your spiritual time might be spent listening to a sermon or a religion-based podcast, praying, walking in nature, visiting a place of worship, doing yoga, or engaging in some sort of Bible study or religious group (though you might need more time for some of these activities).

Ideally your spiritual practice is something you can do without needing childcare and without much planning so you can fit this in as often as you'd like. Consider making it a regular part of your daily or weekly routine, and find the time that works best with your family's needs and schedule. Your family members may be able to participate as well. Maybe you read the Bible or a book that you connect with spiritually aloud as a family, you have a prayer circle together, or you all take time to write in gratitude journals. As with all self-care activities, however, make sure that your spiritual needs are not overshadowed by your family's participation. Young children may struggle with the amount of focus and respect these activities require, so consider if you want your spiritual practice to be a social affair or not.

Work On a Creative Project

Many moms feel energized by spending time on creative projects. However, even if you love to be creative, it's easy to feel overwhelmed when you're forced to come up with some sort of papier-mâché costume on a deadline or asked to cut up teeny tiny squares of paper for a classroom craft. So instead of doing something that doesn't meet your self-care needs, find a project that *you're* interested in.

If it's been a long time since you've done anything crafty or creative, think back to life pre-kids. Did you like to sew, scrapbook, embroider, or do woodworking? If you're still not certain what you'd like to work on, fit in time to head to your local craft store for inspiration. You might already have what you need for this self-care activity (for example, an unfinished scarf still attached to knitting needles from the early 2000s, or a half-done wedding scrapbook), but you might also want to splurge a bit and start something new by buying the materials and tools you need for your project. You likely won't finish in 30 minutes, but having the materials you need on hand may encourage you to get to it, providing emotional and mental self-care more often. You might also find that you can multitask to give you more time to work on your project. For example, if you normally zone out in front of the TV at the end of the day, you can craft while you watch. Find a project for your kids to work on while you do yours. It's a great way for everyone to fit in self-care and also create things to be proud of.

Have Sex

At any point in mom-life it's normal if the thought of sex makes you groan (and not in a good way). As a mom, you spend so much time being needed and touched by your kids that you may find yourself feeling over it by the time your partner wants to be intimate. But the reality is that sexual intimacy is an important part of most couples' relationships, and is one of the keys to staying connected with your partner. It's also related to how you feel about yourself as a woman and can be physical and emotional self-care. For some, sex is a spiritual experience. Now, depending on your love life, this activity could fit in any of our time frames, but it's included in the 30-minute section because for most of us, that's enough time to get the job done well.

If you're pregnant or have a newborn, you have every right to ignore this activity for now, and revisit it later. For everyone else, make sex happen! Consider adding this to your schedule, as frequently as it feels right for your relationship. Spontaneous sex *can* still happen, but you might find it easier to make an "appointment" with your spouse, especially if you have young children. This way, you can mentally and physically prepare, take the steps needed to make sure your children don't interrupt (or choose a time when there is little chance of an interruption, like after bedtime or early morning, if that's your preference), and make the commitment to yourself and your relationship. Many moms feel like scheduling sex actually makes it better, not worse, because without the schedule, it's too easy to put it off.

Get Your Eyebrows Done

Have you ever had the experience where you think, *Hmm, it's been a while since I've had my eyebrows done...well, they're not that bad.* Then you get your eyebrows done, and you realize how amazing you *can* look. There is something about groomed eyebrows that can improve your mood and outlook. But it seems that many women end up skipping their eyebrow appointments once kids enter the picture, and then we're out of the habit.

Remember that practical self-care of this kind, and beauty appointments in general, often leads to positive thoughts and emotions. It's important that you take care of yourself, and a seemingly small detail like amazing eyebrows shouldn't be overlooked. Make the time for this appointment by fitting it in on your lunch break (make sure you don't have any face-to-face meetings planned after lunch that day), or head to work early one day so you can make a late-afternoon appointment. Or find a salon that's close to one of your kids' lessons or appointments and get your eyebrows done while they're busy. If your kids are young, consider bringing them along and have snacks, toys, or coloring books to keep them busy. It may not be ideal to have kids tag along for self-care appointments, but if that's the only way to get them done, do it.

Never had your eyebrows done before? Talk with your local friends about where they go and give it a try. Even a basic cleanup of stray hairs can brighten up your face and your mood.

Work On Your Budget

One of the biggest stresses in life is money. Once you have kids, it can often feel like there's never enough. Though we'd all love to make more money, the reality is that you may be able to get by with what you have if you adjust how you're spending it. So take your 30 minutes and use that time to create a budget for your household.

When creating a household budget you generally want to look at two main things, how much money you have coming in, and how much you have going out. You likely know how much you spend on the big monthly things like rent, cars, and insurance, but sit down with your bank statements from the last couple of months and figure out the averages for your other expenses, like groceries, eating out, entertainment, and clothing. Then figure out what you can actually afford to spend each month and decide how to break that down to cover your family's needs.

While creating a budget can feel restrictive, it can also relieve stress. Challenge yourself to look at it as a plan for *how* you'll spend your money, rather than a plan that *doesn't let you* spend your money. And be sure, if you can, to use this time to include your self-care needs in your budget. Some will be obvious, like having money for self-care activities like manicures and coffee runs, but you also want to account for services like housekeepers and mother's helpers, which will likely be involved in allowing you time for your self-care activities.

Meet Up for Coffee

There's something soothing about drinking coffee or tea on its own, but when you add a friend or two, *and* the fact that you're getting out of the house, this has the ability to turn into fantastic social, mental, and emotional self-care. It's easy to think that you need more than 30 minutes to meet up with a friend, but think about the moms who have similar schedules to you, or friends who have some flexibility to work with your schedule. For example, is there a friend who can grab coffee with you after morning drop-off, before you have to run errands or head to work? Do you have a friend who works nearby and can do a midday pick-me-up with a coffee or visit on your lunch breaks?

These coffee meet-ups can also happen quickly on weekend mornings, so think about adding a coffee break into your weekend routine. For example, if the kids watch cartoons in the morning and your partner is home, meet up with a friend (and bring a coffee back for your partner), or if you normally get out of the house on your own for grocery shopping, extend that time and meet up with a friend. If you can't find time to meet up until later in the day, have decaf. Consider grabbing coffee with your friend and walking with your kids. If your kids are young, bring their strollers, or wear them while you walk. Coffee with a friend is a great way to get social self-care, and if you add a walk, it's physical self-care too!

Have Some Cozy Time

How good does it feel to put on your pajamas or coziest clothes and just relax? *So good*, right? But when's the last time you did that? Use 30 minutes to feel comfortable and enjoy cozying up for some quiet time. This can be the perfect way to create feelings of calm and relaxation, and if you find time for it in the afternoon, it can help you recharge for the rest of your day.

To make the most of this time, put on your most comfortable clothes and find a spot where you can relax: your bed, a chair by a window, or even a spot outdoors. Maybe even get something extra luxurious, like chenille socks or a soft fleece blanket. Be sure that the temperature is appealing to you and that you're physically comfortable in your space, and then read, listen to music, journal, or fill your half hour however you'd like. Your cozy time will be emotional self-care but may also be mental or spiritual self-care, depending on how you spend the time. Your kids might be able to join you for this activity, or you can have your cozy time while they're out of the house or involved in something else. If your kids do join you, just like other self-care activities you include them in, set expectations for their behavior. If they can't stick to the guidelines, they won't be able to join. Help it feel like a privilege to join you in these self-care activities.

Plan a Date Night

Time with your partner is important for your relationship *and* for your mental and emotional self-care. As a parent, you know that dates don't *just happen.* Date night requires planning: sitters, back-up sitters, written plans, and everything organized for your time out. And this doesn't even include the details of the date!

Put 30 minutes on your calendar to tackle the practical side of this self-care task and plan a date that you can go on when you have more time (maybe it's one of the 2–4-hour self-care activities that you'll learn more about in Chapter 7). Look at several options for dates for your date night, reach out to your sitter(s) to see what time they have available, then get it on your calendar! Don't have a sitter? Talk to a friend about swapping time. Remember that dates don't have to be at night. If bedtime is stressful at your house, consider a morning or afternoon date to make it easier on the sitter. This is ultimately easier for you, too, because you won't be sitting at dinner, checking your phone, and wondering if your kids are asleep.

Once you get a date and time on the calendar, start thinking about what you'd like to do. Make a reservation for a restaurant, look at local events, or check sites like *Groupon* and *LivingSocial* for local deals. Basically, do whatever you can to make the stars align, rather than waiting for them to align on their own. (You know that won't happen, so you should check this practical self-care off your list and look forward to your social, emotional, and mental self-care date, even if it's a ways off.)

Add Self-Care to a Chore

Chores are generally not fun. They're tasks we need to complete to help our house and life function. Chores can fall into the category of practical self-care, because you probably feel better when you have them done, like laundry, cleaning, or dishes. But you can enhance these chores by adding another self-care element to them. For example, watch TV while you fold the laundry; call a friend while you're unloading and reloading the dishwasher; or listen to a podcast, audiobook, or music while you're cleaning.

Essentially, this self-care activity gives you an appropriate time to multitask! Chores often have a mindless quality to them (because you've done them over, and over, *and over*), which means you're probably on autopilot and have extra mental capacity to do something else while you're getting the necessities out of the way. You may not *enjoy* your chores, but maybe they become more tolerable this may. You might even finish them more quickly because you're adding an enjoyable element to them. This is also a great way to add more self-care into your routine. If you tend to spend an hour a day on chores, that's an easy place to find an hour for self-care. Encourage your kids to add self-care to their chores too. For example, suggest that they listen to music with headphones while they clean their rooms. This just might lead to less arguing about chores and having them completed more quickly!

Prepare Healthy Snacks

"I'm hungry...can I have a snack?" How often do you hear those words? Maybe constantly. Kids seem to always want snacks, no matter how old they are, and no matter when their last meal took place. While there are so many convenient options that you can grab at the store, buying prepackaged snacks tends to be less cost-effective and it's not always the healthiest route you can take. (But thank goodness for those individually wrapped snacks when you need them!)

When you're at the grocery store, pick up items that all members of your family (including you) can have for snack options. Consider pretzels, nuts, fruit, yogurt, cheese, and veggies with dip. (Purchasing ranch dip, peanut butter, and hummus in individual packages is a great option, but try to buy everything else in larger quantities and portion them out at home.) After your trip to the store use your half-hour self-care time to prepare the snacks. Put items like pretzels and nuts in individual portions and make a place in your pantry where these snacks are easily accessible. Wash fruits and vegetables, cutting them if needed, and have a dedicated space in your fridge for these snacks. This way, not only are all the snacks ready, but your family members know right where to get them and can help themselves, rather than you having to stop what you're doing to find and prepare a snack. And remember, as you learned in "Eat Something" in Chapter 4, being *hangry* is a real thing, so be sure to have healthy options on hand for yourself too.

Pick a Goal and Plan How You'll Get There

Pre-kids, you probably had lots of goals, professional and personal. As children enter the picture, family goals may become the focus, and though your personal goals are still important, they may become harder to reach. But oftentimes goals aren't met because you're missing some of the key elements of effective goal setting.

Use your 30 minutes to choose one goal to focus on. A family-related goal is a fine choice, but challenge yourself to work toward something *you* want. Chances are, this will be a long-term goal, a goal for the future. Decide on a date you'd like to accomplish it by (these deadlines are important), then come up with short-term goals that will help you reach that goal. For example, if you're working toward finishing a DIY project, choose the date you want to have it completed, then determine what you need to have done and in what time frames to reach the long-term goal. Take it one step further, and think about how to reach each short-term goal. This might mean having daily goals where you spend time during the week working toward the goal (it doesn't have to be every day), or possibly strategies you can use to accomplish a goal, such as researching information you need.

When you do this planning, be realistic, especially with your time frame. And if you get off-track, adjust rather than giving up. With the practical self-care of setting your goal, you set yourself up for good feelings as you progress toward, and then accomplish, your goal. Consider sharing your planning and progress with your kids, as this sets a good example about how goals take time and effort, and it shows that your goals are important too.

Get Out of the House

If you're one of the many moms who work from home (either with a paid job or as a stay-at-home mom), you're home…a lot. Sometimes you just need to get away. Even if you work out of the house, you might sometimes feel like you're spending a lot of time at home. And when you do go out, it's typically with your kids and you're on a mission to accomplish something. Plan 30 minutes in your schedule, when you partner is home or when a neighbor can watch the kids, or even when you might be home without the kids but normally would be doing chores, and just leave the house. Take a walk, drive to get coffee, or simply get a chore done, like grabbing some milk.

When we spend too much time at home, even when things are pleasant and running well, being indoors, in the same space all day, can begin to feel suffocating. Changing up your scenery allows for mental and emotional self-care. When you go out, it can be helpful to get some social interaction, even if it means interacting with people you don't know. Whether or not you interact with others, it's useful to remove yourself physically and mentally from your house from time to time. If your kids are young and you have no one to watch them, try to find ways to spend some time outside alone. For example, sit in your backyard or on the front steps while your kids nap. This may not be truly getting away from the house, but this self-care doesn't have to be an all-or-nothing activity.

Connect with Your Partner

Being a parent may make you feel like a fast-moving train. And sometimes your partner isn't even on the same train or schedule as you! Because of that, it's very easy to feel disconnected, and it can be difficult to get back on the same page. By adding in a half hour on a regular basis specifically to reconnect, your relationship (and you) will feel stronger.

The 30 minutes can be spent however you'd like, but go into the time with the focus on connecting. Choose a time when you can be with just each other, with minimal (ideally no) distractions. This might be after the kids go to bed, or when they're at a lesson or practice you're both attending and you can step outside together for a bit. Maybe take the kids to the park or the mall, and while they hang out, you two do the same. During this time share what's going on in your lives, plan for an upcoming date, work through any challenges you're facing, or simply enjoy each other's company.

You might connect over a quick meal, a show, or maybe even folding laundry or cleaning the garage together. There are lots of ways to connect, so brainstorm with your partner about how and when you can do this and then build this important time into your schedules. Remember, your relationship is a priority, and in some ways taking this time is practical self-care because it's one of those things you just need to get done, but more importantly, it's mental, emotional, and social self-care as well.

Organize Clothes for the Week

How often have you told your kids to get dressed and they tell you they can't find anything to wear? Or you're struggling to put together an outfit for them even though you *know* you've done laundry? Taking 30 minutes once (or twice) a week to plan outfits can help get your family organized. This practical self-care can lead to more peaceful mornings and a better mood for everyone. Come up with a system that works for your family, and organize *your* weekly outfits, too, if you think that will help.

Put together complete outfits, something that covers the top and the bottom, along with underwear and socks. Put these outfits in drawers or baskets, or simply have them lined up on the dresser. Also, have a central location for shoes and outerwear. Then, when it comes time to get dressed, your child picks an outfit and puts it on (or you pick one and help them get dressed). This can help to avoid fights in the morning over what to wear, along with the issue of not being able to find clothes. If your kids are old enough, work with them to plan outfits on their own at the start of the week, allowing them to take ownership of the process. Though this may not solve all of the problems associated with getting dressed, it can help many of them. Add this into your weekly routine, and commit to getting at least five days of outfits ready for each child in your home.

Take a Bath

You'll need some strategic planning to make sure a bath happens without interruption, but this self-care routine can be the ultimate way to relax and unwind. If your kids tend to go to bed without issue (as in, no requests for water and they don't get up), your kids are older and hang quietly in their rooms in the evening, or you have a partner home at bedtime, taking a bath right after your kids wrap up their day can be a very nice way to transition out of mom mode. Or, if you struggle with shutting down at bedtime, take a bath right before you get into bed (and no phones or screens once you're tucked in!).

To make your bath extra luxurious, add scented bubbles or bath salts, place candles around the room, and even turn on music you enjoy. Get a bath pillow or use a towel to keep your head and neck comfortable. You can also use this time to go through a guided meditation or practice mindfulness (but don't fall asleep!). If you love reading, this is a prime opportunity for that (get one of those bathtub book holders), or listen to an audiobook while you soak. Taking a bath is emotional self-care but may be mental self-care too. Depending on your mood (and the size of your tub), you could even invite your partner in for social self-care, but there's no need to add anyone else to this experience!

Research Life Hacks

All moms have areas of life that they struggle with. For you, it might be dishes. You always have a sink full, whereas your friend never seems to have a visible dirty dish. Ever wonder how your friends tackle things that you find so challenging? Chances are, they have systems in place to make life easier; they've discovered "life hacks" to help simplify and streamline. Take 30 minutes to research hacks that you and your family can use to make life easier. *Google* and *Pinterest* are great resources and can help you find solutions for anything from cleaning and organization to meal prep, budgeting, and more.

After all, there's no need to continue to struggle when there might be a simple solution or strategy you haven't thought of. Sometimes small changes can help you get through your daily and weekly tasks with more ease, and other times you'll need a larger overhaul. Making changes, both large and small, can help you and your family reduce stress and save time. Rather than trying to improve everything at once, pick one area, such as laundry, and research time-saving tips, routines, and "life hacks," and then plan for how you can apply what you've learned. It might take a little time to get your new system in place, but it's worth it to spend time on this practical self-care.

Chapter 6

1-Hour Activities

One hour. Just imagine what you can do with a full hour to yourself! The list of possibilities will continue to grow when you set aside 60 minutes for self-care. You'll notice that more of the activities take place out of the house, because it's more realistic to get away when you have an hour. Yes, this means that childcare or coordinating with your partner will be part of the equation, but it will be worth it. Why? Because when you're able to spend more time practicing self-care, you're more likely to be able to hit on several types of self-care within one activity. And you can also add social self-care to a few of the activities in this chapter even if it isn't explicitly stated. If you can—and want to—include a friend or family member in your self-care, you may find that it helps to enhance the experience. Remember, if you're not used to setting aside an hour for yourself, it will feel strange, and you may experience guilt at first. But stick with it! Remind yourself that you're worth it, and that everyone is better off when you take care of yourself. And with 168 hours in a week, it's okay to take an hour here and there.

Have a Self-Care Family Meeting

With all the self-care you're going to be doing, you want to make sure your family understands the importance of the time you'll be taking for yourself. So it's helpful to have a self-care family meeting to get everyone on the same page (or at least close to it) about the importance of self-care.

Use part of your hour to prep for your meeting, and the rest of the time to sit down and talk with your family. Start by explaining what self-care is, and the benefits (refer to Chapter 1 if you need to), and talk about how you're a better person, mom, partner, employee, etc. when you're taking care of yourself. You can also help your family think about how they take care of themselves and about what would happen if they didn't do those self-care activities.

Once you help your family understand its importance, move on to the practicalities of your self-care. You don't have to tell them all the activities involved in self-care, but it's probably helpful to mention that you'll be setting aside more time for yourself as well as the expectations for behavior when this is happening. For example, set boundaries like no barging into your room before seven thirty in the morning because you'll be journaling, or that when you're doing dishes you'll be listening to your music, so no requests allowed. Essentially, you want to help set the stage so your family is supportive of the time you'll be making for yourself. You can also help family members plan their own self-care activities so everyone gets their "me" time.

Take an Exercise Class

Physical exercise is such an important part of your self-care, health, and overall well-being. Joining a gym, with an instructor to guide and motivate you, can be a great way to change up your routine and get in a good workout. Even if you don't belong to a gym, you can typically get a free pass to a club or specialty studio to try it out. Or you can find an inexpensive membership or class package through sites like *Groupon* and *LivingSocial*. Some gyms even offer childcare so that the kids can go with you. If going to the gym becomes part of your self-care routine, childcare often becomes something the kids look forward to as part of their social self-care!

Not sure what kind of class to take? If you love music and moving your body, a dance-based class might be for you. If you want something calmer, then yoga or Pilates could be a good choice. If you already work out and typically do cardio, consider trying a weight-lifting class. You might even want to ask a friend to join you to add in some social self-care along with your physical self-care. If you're feeling uncertain about doing a workout class, remember that the people in the room are usually looking at themselves and not you. Consider bringing a friend with you to help quell your nerves. Then you can grab a post-workout smoothie or coffee together if you have some extra time.

Meet a Friend for Lunch

When you end up with an hour in your schedule, getting together with a friend for social self-care is a great choice. You'll probably need to plan this one in advance to make sure it happens. Meet up with a friend during your lunch break at work, or invite a friend over while your little ones nap. If you have to be strict with the hour timeline, be sure to choose a friend who can be punctual. Find a meeting place that doesn't require too much travel time, and consider choosing a restaurant where you can order at the counter and food is cooked more quickly, rather than meeting at a sit-down restaurant where there can be delays and you risk feeling rushed and stressed.

If you're meeting another mom, challenge yourselves to talk about what's going on for you, your feelings and experiences. Though this conversation may include some talk of your kids, it should be more about what's going on for *you*. If your lunch includes another mom with kids who are not in school yet, be clear about whether you're okay with the younger kids tagging along. In some situations this might be fine. A small baby may sleep or be content at lunch, whereas toddlers may not allow this time to feel like self-care, even if they aren't your kids. If your lunch date ends up being canceled, use this time to pick another 1-hour activity for yourself and reschedule your lunch for another day.

Delegate to Your Children

It's a fact that moms take on *a lot* of the household chores. Even if you have a partner who is helpful, you still have a lot to do. You may avoid delegating chores and tasks to your children because the kids "don't do it well enough" or it's a fight to get them to do their chores, but kids can usually get involved at a younger age than we think. And if your kids are older, it's never too late to start. So give it a try! You'll be less likely to feel resentment when others help at home, you'll have more time and energy for other things, and you'll be helping to prepare your kids for life beyond your home.

Pick one or two tasks for your kids to take on (you can add more once these become habits). If you're not sure what's appropriate, google chores for your child's age and remember that even toddlers can help with simple tasks. Explain to your kids that as members of the household, everyone pitches in. Show the task to your child, explaining the steps and allowing them to watch you complete it a few times before they take over. Then have them practice. Resist the urge to "fix" it or make it better. This sends the message that the job they did wasn't good enough. Instead, teach them how to improve and how to do their job well. Remember, done is better than perfect, and in time they'll get better at it.

Get Your Nails Done

As you learned in "Paint Your Nails" in Chapter 4, having your nails painted can give even the most frenzied mom a put-together look, and getting an hour-long manicure is a treat that's even more welcome! Chances are, unless you go for shellac or acrylic nails, your polish from a manicure won't last long. But don't let that stop you from enjoying the pampering that comes from a manicure or pedicure involving a hand or foot soak, massage, moisturizing, and more. Not only can you zone out while someone else tends to your needs, but you can enjoy additional self-care while you relax and listen to some music or a podcast or catch up on some reading. Even better, make this into a social self-care experience by inviting a friend or two.

If your budget allows, a mani and a pedi together are a fantastic treat. When you book your appointment, request that you get both treatments at the same time so that you have enough time for both. If they can't accommodate you and you need to do one at a time, ask for a quick-dry top coat. If you love getting a manicure but hate chipped nails, choose a subtle color so that the chips aren't as obvious, or go for a clear or shimmer color.

Remember that most nail salons can accommodate walk-ins, so this is a great self-care activity to do spontaneously. You can also use this time for practical self-care. Get a pedicure and keep your hands free to respond to emails, do your meal planning, or get some work done. Or don't! Your self-care is up to you!

Sleep In

Remember those days, pre-kids, when nothing had to happen first thing in the morning? There was no one demanding that you get up, and you could just sleep? Ahh, memories. Sleeping in can feel like an indulgent (and needed) way to spend an hour of your time. As moms, we are usually running on not enough sleep.

Your inner clock will likely wake you up at your usual time, but be willing to close your eyes, breathe deeply, and fall back asleep. Consider a sleep mask if you normally wake up with the sun. If your time frame for this extra sleep is strict, you may want to set an alarm, because once your body returns to sleep, it may not wake up naturally at the exact time you'd like.

Sleeping in will take coordination and support from the members of your family. If you have older kids who tend to sleep in on the weekends, this is a good time for you to put aside early-morning tasks and do the same. If, however, you have young kids, or early risers, see about getting your partner on board to assist with keeping the kids quiet or out of the house so that you can sleep. Return the favor for your partner on another day. If you fly solo in the mornings, you'll need to be more strategic with this self-care option. The ages of your kids will influence how you plan, but consider setting up a breakfast station for your kids, make sure they have activities to keep them busy, or teach them how to turn on the TV.

Go to a Doctor's Appointment

You're probably on top of it with your kid's doctors' appointments: dentist twice a year, an eye exam, and an annual physical with the pediatrician at the minimum. Some families also have appointments with specialists, due to a child's disability or chronic illness. Managing and attending these appointments can take up a lot of time. Because of this, you may be canceling or avoiding your own appointments. This needs to stop. Your family is better off with you being healthy, and you send a bad message to them when you don't take your doctors' appointments seriously.

With one hour you can get a doctor's appointment over and done with. Yes, you'll have to schedule it in advance, but once it's on your calendar, consider it to be an appointment with yourself and don't break it. You know that doctors typically run later as the day progresses, so try for the earliest appointment possible, and be prepared with an audiobook, laptop, tablet, etc. so that you can make the most of any time spent waiting.

Also, bring your calendar with you so that you can schedule your next appointment while you're there. That way, you won't have to spend mental energy remembering to make the appointment later, or feel badly that you've put it off. Consider scheduling your yearly exams around your birthday so they're easier to remember. Get into this habit so that your practical self-care is prioritized and happens on a regular basis. You'll be glad you did.

Go to Church or a Place of Worship

If you are a mom who is religious, going to church can be one of the strongest ways to fulfill your spiritual self-care needs. And it's highly likely that your visit will also allow for mental, emotional, and possibly social self-care as well. Church can be a rewarding family experience, but the ages and attention spans of your children may negatively influence your ability to focus, connect, and worship in the way that's important to you. Consider attending church alone if you can, or utilize childcare if it's offered. If you must bring your young children along and your partner attends church, too, devise a plan so that both of you are able to have your spiritual needs met. For example, one week, if the kids are fussy, you leave with them, and the next week your partner leaves. Though this might not be the ideal solution, at least you have a plan for how to handle the interruptions. If there is no support and attending a service is too challenging, consider going to church at any time that works for you to sit silently and worship. You may want to attend a service, but if there are too many barriers, don't let them keep you away from church altogether.

If you haven't attended church before, or you consider yourself spiritual as opposed to religious, do some research to find a church or place of worship that matches your spiritual beliefs. Remember that everyone's spiritual needs are different, and that's true for your kids as well. If it's important to you, don't let the beliefs of other family members get in the way of you being able to attend church or your place of worship.

Unplug

We are around technology constantly, and it can improve life in many ways. Technology can help us stay more organized, there are apps that help with self-care, and we can improve our connection with others. However, there is also the chance of being too connected. It's easy to waste time on social media or by playing mindless games. This is the downside to technology. As a mom, you may monitor your children's screen time and Internet use, but do you monitor yours? Give it a try! Take an hour and just unplug. This will help you become more in tune with yourself, and be more present. Unplugging can be uncomfortable at first, so this may need to start as a 15-minute activity, but work your way up to an hour or even more.

What you do while you unplug is up to you, but the goal is to go an hour without technology—no phone, no Internet, and even no TV or music. Cut out all electronics if you like, including your microwave! Be brave and actually turn off your phone. Yes, that's hard as a mom, but it can be worthwhile. Remember the time before cell phones? We were all okay. You can stay solo for your time unplugged, but hanging out as a family without your devices is a good habit to create that will benefit everyone. Connect with your family, creating emotional and social self-care. Try heading outside together for a walk or to play ball, or simply pull out a board game and play together.

Get a Massage

A massage might be a self-care cliché, but it's a great way to spend an hour. So book yourself a massage (with a bit of extra time for relaxing before and after, if you can), and enjoy. Many moms find it difficult to turn off their minds, and end up thinking about chores, tasks, and things they need to do instead taking this time to relax. Resist this urge! Instead, focus on your breathing, or on the sensations of the muscles being rubbed. Your massage can also happen with a friend in the room, which means you'll get some social self-care along with your mental and emotional self-care.

If you're hesitant because of the nudity involved, remember that 1) you're beautiful, 2) you don't have to be completely naked, and 3) a masseuse is a professional and sees bodies of all shapes and sizes. Also, you can do different types of massage, such as feet or arms and neck; you don't have to do a full-body massage if you don't want to. But they are amazing. Go for it! If a massage feels like too much of a splurge (they can get expensive!), look for deals on sites like *Groupon* or *LivingSocial,* check for coupons or discounts on local spa websites, or ask for a gift certificate for the next gift-giving holiday. You might even find a location that sells packages, allowing you to get a monthly massage at an affordable rate.

Evaluate How Work Fits Into Your Life

Maybe you work a full-time job that you enjoy but wish there was more flexibility. Perhaps you work part time and hate it. Maybe you don't work outside the home and love that, or you don't work and miss it. Regardless of your current situation, take time to reflect on work and how it currently fits into your life. Consider what your work-life balance looks like now, how it affects your family life, and if you'd prefer it to be different.

Often, working moms feel like they have a lot on their plate at all times. If you don't work, you have a lot going on, too, and if you're considering going back to work, that would mean another set of responsibilities and potentially more sources of stress. It would also mean less time to devote to being a mom and taking care of yourself. During this hour of reflection, consider how you can fit in self-care as a working mom (refer to the 5- and 15-minute activities in Chapters 3 and 4), as well as ways to simplify your life or improve routines so that you can feel calmer at home. And if you're not working but would like to, use this time to consider how and when you might be able to fit work back into your life. This is practical self-care, in that you're reflecting and planning. The goal is to create room for self-care even as a working mom, as well as figure out how to have less stress.

Catch Up on Your Favorite Show

Sometimes TV becomes a mindless way to spend your time. You're exhausted, so you turn it on and check out. While that's fine, watching something that you actually enjoy can be emotional self-care. Also, since some TV *can* be intellectually stimulating, it can be mental self-care too. So don't feel guilty! Be intentional with your TV time, and watch something you love.

Pick a show you've seen before, or maybe find a new one to start watching (ask your friends for recommendations). It can be fun to find a special show for you and your partner to watch together. Doing this provides some social self-care along with building a connection and nurturing your relationship with your partner.

With an hour, you can watch two or three episodes of a half-hour show (fast-forward through the commercials if you can), or a full one-hour show from start to finish. Do your best to find a time when you won't be interrupted, then put your phone away and enjoy. You can turn this into multitasking time if you plan ahead (but you don't have to!). For example, fold laundry while you watch. This way you're also getting in some practical self-care, but it won't take away from the experience of enjoying your show. As your kids get older, depending on the type of TV you like to watch, you might be able to share this time with them.

Plan for Your Week

Mom-life can be overwhelming, often because of the amount of stuff we have to do: drop-offs, pick-ups, practices, events, appointments, lessons, and playdates. And that doesn't even include your own tasks, responsibilities, and chores! At the beginning of the week, before everything gets into full swing, sit down with your calendar (paper, wall, digital, or all of the above) and take a look at what you have going on. Even when your schedule is similar week-to-week, it's still a good idea to reassess each week, so nothing slips through the cracks.

Make sure you have all the drop-offs and pick-ups accounted for, and look at the lessons, game schedules, and other activities to make sure there are no unexpected conflicts that need to be addressed. Get in the habit of adding all appointments, invites, and activities to your calendar as soon as you get them. That way you'll know right away if there are conflicts, and since they're on the calendar, things won't be forgotten and missed. Think about doing self-care planning at this point, too, because you'll be able to see where you may have time available. Over time, you may not need a full hour for this activity, but it's useful to have this time available. If you have the family's calendar organized and your self-care plan is done, you can use any remaining time for meal planning, organizing your grocery list, getting kids' clothes together, or any other organizational tasks that help you be prepared for the week. Consider adding this time into your schedule every week. As your kids get older, have them take ownership of their own tasks to encourage their learning and use of organization and scheduling skills.

Volunteer

Giving your time is good for the soul, it benefits you, and it's meaningful to whomever you help and serve. Volunteering can be anything: helping at your kids' school or with their sports teams, cleaning up trash, helping at an animal shelter, or visiting a senior center. Your children's school likely has information on volunteer opportunities, or you can look up local organizations or causes that interest you. Most organizations have web pages with information for volunteers. If they don't, give them a call and ask.

Consider your skills, talents, and interests when you look for volunteer opportunities. For example, if you have a background in design, you could help a local charity design flyers for an upcoming event, or if sewing or knitting is your specialty, find a local hospital that needs blankets or hats for sick babies and children. Not only do you experience mental and emotional self-care when you volunteer, but these activities may provide additional self-care. Some volunteer activities can be done at home and still be helpful, like sewing and knitting or stuffing envelopes, which is great if you're interested in volunteering but your availability doesn't match when the location is open.

Keep in mind that some organizations require training and background checks in order to volunteer. Others allow you to drop in and help anytime, or schedule an hour at a time without training. Be sure to check into the volunteer requirements when you do your research. If you'd like your children to join you, consider researching locations together to help them become invested in the process and boost their interest.

Go to a Nursery

If you're looking for a fantastic hour-long self-care activity, head over to a nursery. No, not a baby nursery (though for some, that might be enjoyable too!). I mean the kind of nursery where you find flowers, plants, and other items for your yard or home. A nursery provides an amazing sensory experience. Taking the time to enjoy the sight of the beautiful flowers and foliage, listen to the various sounds that are present, and savor the smells can be emotional self-care. The act of walking through and really noticing what's around forces you to be in the present moment, which will provide mental self-care and, for some, can be a spiritual experience. And whether you visit a dedicated nursery or the plant section of your local hardware store, you can likely learn while you're there. Many stores have informational literature about the plants, and some have educational exhibits and classes, which means more mental self-care.

This activity may be one to bring your children to. Depending on their ages, you can organize a scavenger hunt for them to do while they're at the nursery. For example, have them find five items that are purple, ten leaves that look different, or a plant or flower for every letter of the alphabet. This way, you can have your own experience while your kids are close by and occupied; the autonomy is great for everyone. At the end of your visit, bring home a small potted plant or flowers to remind you of the experience, or go home empty-handed. You don't need to worry about keeping one more thing alive, unless you really want to.

Attend Therapy or a Support Group

You have a lot going on in your life. Even with the love and encouragement of a partner, family, and friends, sometimes different support—like therapy or a support group—can be beneficial. Some people believe therapy or counseling is only for large struggles or mental health disorders, but that's not all therapy assists with. Yes, if you're struggling, therapy can be a huge help. But therapy is also a place to go to help you identify what's working, reflect with an unbiased individual, and help you focus on yourself. Some women love counseling sessions and go regularly even when nothing is "wrong," because it's time to think about themselves. Working with a therapist is mental and emotional self-care and helps to ensure that you take the time for you. Sometimes these sessions will be emotional and you'll tackle the hard topics, but you'll do so in a space where you are supported.

Group support is another way to get encouragement, and it can be useful if you or someone you love is dealing with a challenging life circumstance or health issue. For example, there are support groups related to being a new mom, breastfeeding, anxiety, parenting teens, and more. These groups include other individuals with the same challenge, concerns, or life circumstances, and a leader who is trained in the topic you're meeting about. You can usually find out about support groups through your insurance company, doctor's office, or local hospital, or just take a look online for other options. There may even be online support groups, but meeting in person enhances your social self-care.

Have a Beauty Hour

This self-care activity is all about prioritizing yourself and your beauty for a full hour. You can make this about your inner beauty by doing some journaling or affirmations, or about your outer beauty by painting your nails or doing your hair. The idea is that you spend an hour, likely at home, maybe with a friend, focusing on activities that help you feel beautiful. This could be a shorter version of the at-home spa session (see "Create an At-Home Spa Session" in Chapter 7), but it can allow you to combine a few different shorter self-care activities as well.

If you plan this hour before a night out with friends or before a date night with your partner, it can increase the excitement for going out and help you get out of the mom frame of mind to focus on yourself as a person. Though you probably don't *need* an hour to get ready, how nice would it be to take the time for yourself, to not be rushed, and to leave the house feeling good? To have the time you want, be sure to communicate with your partner—or whoever will be watching the kids—that this is your time! (Maybe get a "do not disturb" sign for the door!) If the kids can be out of the house for the hour, even better. Or if you have kids who are old enough and might be able to participate in some of the activities of your beauty hour, invite them to join in to get their own emotional self-care.

Do a Walk and Talk

Making the time to catch up with friends is important self-care, and adding in a walk allows you to get physical activity while getting out of the house. Coordinating schedules can sometimes be a challenge, so keep in mind that your friend doesn't have to physically be with you; you can talk on the phone while you walk (use headphones to avoid getting a stiff neck). Also, if you have an older child with a class or lesson, check if there's a walking path close by. You don't need to watch every single class or practice, and this is a good way to make use of that time. This is also a great activity for your lunch break during the workday. Consider creating a standing appointment with a friend to get in regular socializing and physical activity.

This is a self-care activity that's perfect for when your kids are young and still in a stroller, or when you can wear them in a baby carrier or wrap. Toddlers may enjoy this as well, so load up the stroller with snacks and toys to keep them occupied. If you can, choose a location where you'll see people on bikes or walking with dogs—this can help keep your kids entertained—so you can enjoy chatting with your friend(s).

Do That Thing You Keep Meaning to Do

We all have a thing (or many) that we keep *meaning* to do, but don't. It might be dealing with a pile of papers, finishing the baby book, sorting through old clothes, cleaning out the car, or even tackling a much bigger project. Most often, it's a practical task or chore that we don't enjoy doing, and because we keep putting it off, we feel annoyed, guilty, or frustrated. We likely also continue to think about it until it's completed.

With an hour, commit to completing (or chipping away) at that thing that's hanging over your head. Not only does this feel like mental self-care (goodbye, nagging negativity) and emotional self-care (hello, positive emotions for taking this on), but if this is a big task, you're probably going to create some momentum to complete it sooner rather than later. Depending on what the *thing* is, consider how you can make it more enjoyable. For example, listen to music or an audiobook as you sort through a pile, or call a friend while you clean out the car. If the task is mentally or emotionally taxing and an hour at a time is too much, break it into smaller chunks, but get started. You'll feel good about the progress and will likely want to keep going.

Go Shopping—Alone

The idea for this practical self-care task is that you should head out and run errands on your own. There's nothing like errands without kids to make you feel *very* efficient (while also making you realize how much kids can slow you down!). If you're going to use this hour for several errands, make a list of what needs to get done, consider the order that makes the most sense (stop by a coffee shop to make this a little more luxurious), and then get to it.

Or just go to the store! By yourself. Make your list, grab a coffee or drink when you get there, and stroll around. Leisurely stroll through the aisles, grabbing what you need while also checking out any other amazingness that the store offers, like in the home décor section. If you have a little extra money that you can spend while you're shopping, consider picking up something new for your self-care, like a book, nail polish, a face scrub, or scented candles. Use this time to shop at a more relaxed pace, check things off your list, and enjoy your time.

Be sure to pay attention to what you put in your cart though! We've all had shopping trips that start off as diapers and toothpaste, or dog-food and toilet cleaner, or batteries and light bulbs (you get the point), and $100 later you're leaving the store wondering how it happened again. As amazing as shopping can be, especially when you're flying solo, you don't want to experience the post-spending hangover.

Go On a Bike Ride

Riding a bike gives you physical exercise (even if you ride at a leisurely pace), and allows you to get outdoors and experience new sights and sounds. Take the time to plan your route, making sure you have a safe place to ride, and that there aren't unexpected challenges, like a very hilly area if you're looking for an enjoyable cruise. You might look for a local lake or reservoir with a bike path, a quiet neighborhood, or open trails. Be sure to pack water and snacks for your ride.

You may find exercising outdoors to be more enjoyable than other ways to get in your physical activity (and riding your bike may not *feel* as much like exercise). In addition to the physical self-care, you're likely to experience pleasant scenery and enjoy your time, which means this is also emotional self-care. Being outdoors can also be spiritual self-care for some moms. A bike ride can be a good self-care activity to include your family in (scooters or other modes of transportation can work well for the kids too), and a weekly or monthly bike ride can be a worthwhile addition to your family's self-care routine.

Do a Self-Care Grab Bag

A self-care grab bag is when you pick your favorite 5-, 15-, or 30-minute self-care activities and string them together. To do this, plan an hour in your schedule, and decide what you want to do for yourself. If you're the type of person who gets overwhelmed with choices, plan not only the time, but also which activities you'll do. Or, if you like to be spontaneous, decide what you're in the mood for when the time comes. Challenge yourself to include as many types of self-care as you can.

This hour can be used for some of your favorite self-care activities, or can be a time when you try something new. Consider inviting a friend to join you to ensure you get some social self-care in as well. Remember that self-care can be done any time of day, so if you're struggling to find time during the day, schedule your grab-bag hour for right after your kids go to bed or the hour before you go to sleep, and focus on activities that help you feel relaxed and put you in the mood for sleep. Schedule a self-care grab bag whenever you like, and in other increments of time, but remember that adding shorter self-care activities together creates more impact.

Visit an Animal Shelter

Check with your local shelter to see if you can volunteer or simply find out their visitor hours, then head out for some mental and emotional self-care. This visit isn't about looking for your next pet, so if you don't want to bring home a new family member, you may not want to invite the kids to come along. Instead, going to an animal shelter is about connecting with the animals, quieting your mind, and having a positive sensory experience. Animals are sometimes used as a part of therapy because they can help quell anxiety and nerves, and can help you feel calmer and more at peace.

This visit is also about giving back to the animals. Many of them are looking for their forever homes and may not get many visitors. You can help to improve their mood and experience while they wait to meet their new families. When you visit, talk to the employees about your goals. Are you looking to sit quietly? Perhaps you can pet and brush the cats. If you're feeling energetic, maybe you can take a dog for a walk or play with the animals outside. Enjoy the experience, and take a selfie or a video that you can look at later when you need a little pick-me-up.

Take a Nap

Being a mom is exhausting. Even when you've gotten through the newborn phase, the sleep regressions, and the transition out of the crib, and your kids are *really* sleeping through the night, it's normal to still be tired. You're on the go a lot, juggling responsibilities, schedules, and more, so being tired is normal, even as your kids get older. Lack of sleep can cause crankiness, less control over emotions, poor food choices (man, that cookie looks good!), and less effectiveness in whatever it is that we have to do. So during a week when you're feeling especially overwhelmed, or perhaps your kids have woken up in the night more than usual, have gotten up too early, or have kept you up with late-night study sessions, make an hour in your schedule to simply take a nap.

During the week, depending on the ages of your kids, you might be able to do this while your kids are at home, doing homework or playing quietly. Or perhaps you can coordinate with a friend to have the kids at her house for an hour after school and you can rest at home. If you're working all day, choose an evening when your partner can be solely responsible for the kids when you all get home so you can get your nap in. If this can't happen during the week, the weekend can work too. If you're new to napping, you may find it's a struggle to quiet your mind and fall asleep. Try some deep breathing or meditation to relax and prepare you for your nap. Adult napping is a skill that will improve over time, so keep trying.

Go On a Mini-Date

It's too easy to put off going on dates because you don't have enough time. But take away the traditional assumption that a date requires a lot of time and instead think about having mini-dates when you can. The focus and intention, not the amount of time, make the date meaningful. And though we have longer dates covered in Chapter 7, mini-dates are an important way to connect with your partner, and provide important mental and emotional self-care.

Your mini-date can take place at home. For example, spend an hour stargazing or enjoy a meal together after the kids go to bed. If your kids are old enough, it can be fun to have them be your waitstaff for this date. But even with just an hour, you should try to get out of the house. Choose a restaurant where you order from the counter. If you work close enough to each other, schedule a long lunch and meet up midday. Or have a date while your child is at a lesson or an after-school activity. You might even find that on the weekends it's easier to trade childcare with friends because you're only asking for an hour.

If you and your partner are quite busy, it's tempting to use this time to catch up on logistics and what's happening with the kids; resist the urge! Instead, spend this time connecting (or reconnecting) with each other and focus on topics that build the relationship. Discuss your future, reminisce about life pre-kids, and remember who you are as individuals and as a couple.

Schedule Your Appointments

How many times have you thought, *I need to schedule [car mainte-nance, a haircut, a dentist appointment, or a teacher conference...all of the appointments]*? It's generally simple to make appointments, but it's also an easy task to put off. So end the cycle of *I need to sched-ule...* and make an hour-long appointment with yourself to *make appointments* (though it might not take that long and then you can use the remaining time as you'd like). This is practical self-care but will probably be mental self-care, too, because you won't have to think about scheduling the appointments anymore.

Start off with a list of the appointments you and your family members need, along with those the household requires (like main-tenance checks for the car, or installation of home appliances). Then pull out your calendar and start getting things booked! If you can, set up these appointments online; that way you don't have to go back and forth with the scheduling person. Once any online appointments have been made, work on scheduling the ones that require more work, like calling or emailing anyone (like private coaches) who you have to coordinate with. Keep in mind that you may not want to make these calls around lunch, as many offices take breaks and you'll end up having to call back. Though you might not have everything set at the end of this hour, you'll likely have most of them scheduled, and then you can set aside a few minutes here and there in your schedule to get the others done.

Join or Start a Book Club

A book club can be the ultimate way to practice both mental and social self-care. Generally, book clubs choose a book to read together, and then meet up to discuss it. These get-togethers typically include food and drinks and conversation that goes beyond the book discussion, so you can make connections with new people, even if you don't know anyone when you join.

A positive thing about book clubs is that they help hold you accountable for getting your reading done, which means you're getting support to accomplish your self-care. Knowing that you have a date on the calendar to meet with others for socializing can help create positive emotions leading up to the book club meeting. Even though scheduling may be tough, book clubs tend to meet on designated days and times, so you'll be able to plan for childcare.

Virtual book clubs are also an option if you're finding it a challenge to get to meetings. And with a virtual book club, you're not constrained by geography, so you can even reach out to your friends who live in other areas to see about starting a book club together. Start with one or two other people, choose a book you'd all like to read, come up with a day and time that works for everyone, and use an app like Skype or Google Hangouts to meet up and chat about the book (and life).

Create and Use a Babysitting Co-op

A babysitting co-op is where you work with a group of friends with similarly aged kids, ideally four families, and one night each weekend all of the kids are brought to one house to be cared for and the other parents have that time off. This means that once a month you have a house full of kids, and three times a month you have time for yourself with your partner (or without). Amazing, right?! If this setup works, it can be a game changer for making sure you get regular nights out.

For a co-op to function well, create clear guidelines. For example, babies must be at least nine months old to join (before that time, parents could drop off older children, but the babies stay with the parents). You want to make sure that the other parents in the co-op are people you trust and that the kid dynamic will work. If you and your friends have a lot of kids, or there are a lot of young children, you may also want to include a sitter to assist (or pay an older sibling to help with the childcare duties). There would also need to be a contingency plan for when the babysitting family has an emergency on the night they're meant to host.

You can search for "babysitting co-op" online to get more information on ways to set this up, which apps can help you, and how to create a co-op that runs smoothly and is a positive experience for everyone involved. Setting up a co-op is practical self-care with a high payoff. You'll have time for all sorts of self-care while your kids enjoy time with the other families. So take an hour to create your co-op, then use this time for your 2–4-hour activities.

Part 3

Extended Self-Care Activities

In addition to the self-care activities you can do daily (or most days of the week), it's also important that we moms take more than an hour at a time for ourselves. Though this extended self-care may not happen weekly, you can probably fit one of the 2–4-hour activities from Chapter 7 into your schedule at least monthly, and one of the goal activities from Chapter 8 in quarterly or once or twice a year.

You may find yourself doing the longer self-care activities found in this section less often, but remember that you're worth this time, and be sure to make it happen. These activities *will* require more planning, coordination, and support from others, but don't let these things become barriers. Extended self-care activities will remind you of who you are as a woman and a person, give you the time and space to connect with yourself (and others) in important ways, and allow you to step back into being a mom with renewed energy. Let's check them out.

Chapter 7

2–4-Hour Activities

Self-care that lasts more than an hour feels indulgent. No matter what you do with that time, taking it is special and shows that you value yourself. The challenge is that it's not always easy to make a longer stretch of time happen, so make sure that you put these activities on your calendar, monthly if possible, and enlist a sitter or your older kids, or swap sitting with a friend, to make sure extended self-care happens. Remember, you shouldn't feel guilty for taking this time. It's important to you and everyone around you that your self-care happens in more than just bit-sized chunks of time. (And let's face it, anything that lasts 60 minutes or less is over before we know it. Yes, it's still effective, but it often feels like it's over much too quickly!) When you take a few hours to yourself, you can walk back into mom-life feeling renewed and prepared. Since these activities take more time, it also makes it clear to others that you're prioritizing yourself, and this is a strong message to all the people in your life—including your kids.

Go to a Movie

When's the last time you saw a movie? In a theater? That wasn't a cartoon or rated PG? It's probably been a while. Chances are, before kids, you went to the movies. Or if you didn't actually *go* to the movies often, you probably watched them at home not long after they became available. As a mom, you may struggle to find the time to actually watch a movie. But it's so enjoyable to sit back, watch something *you* are interested in, and get lost in a story for a couple of hours. For this activity, you can watch a movie at home, but try to do it when you won't be interrupted (like during your kids' nap time, if those are long enough in your house), or after the kids are in bed (if you can stay awake!).

If you're the kind of person who prefers to get out, plan to go to the movie theater. Bonus points if you have a theater where you can reserve your ticket, sit in a chair that reclines, and order food and drinks from your seat. But even a no-frills theater will do. Decide if you'd like to go on your own (sometimes this is easiest because you can work around your schedule, you can choose a movie *you* want to see, and you don't have to share your snacks), but this can also be a great activity to include your partner, a friend, or another loved one. Depending on your interests and the ages of your kids, this could also be an activity where you bring them along for. But if you do, make sure it's a movie *you* want to see that's also appropriate for your kiddo(s).

Have a Leisurely Meal
with Someone You Love

Kids can make mealtime fun, but *relaxing* and *leisurely* are not the words we usually use to describe meals with kids until they're practically adults. With your 2–4 hours of self-care, revisit the days, pre-children, when you didn't have to rush through a meal. Plan a time with a friend, adult family member, partner, or other loved one(s), and take time to sit, enjoy each other's company, and have a leisurely meal. Go out to eat, or have a meal at home after the kids go to bed, and consider ordering in so you don't have to cook or make a mess (that you'll then have to clean!).

If you go to a restaurant, let your server know you're not in a rush, order a salad or appetizer and drinks first, and then place your main course order. If you're dining at a fast-paced restaurant, or you feel that the staff are looking for you to move on, head to the bar or lounge to continue your visit. Or go to a local coffee shop for dessert. The idea is that you move at a slower, more intentional pace, both through your meal and through your time with your loved one, so that you have a meaningful experience that takes care of many of your self-care needs.

Take a Painting Class

Even if you're not artistic, you can be a painter. Look for an art studio that hosts classes where you're led through painting a specific picture by a trained instructor. These classes are usually set up as "paint and drink," but you don't need to include the alcohol. There are a few things that make painting classes a strong choice for self-care:

1. It can become a social experience by including your friends, but even if you go alone, you'll meet other people, and the teachers tend to be friendly and engaging, interacting with you as you paint.

2. You get to tap into your creative side. Even if you lack confidence in your ability, the classes are designed to take you through the painting process step by step, allowing you to walk away feeling proud of what you've created, which means this is emotional self-care.

3. Painting also stimulates your mind, so check off mental self-care too.

4. You'll produce something concrete, which you can then place in your home to show that you are a person who creates things (other than kids!), which can help you to continue to feel positively about yourself.

Look for discounted classes on sites like *Groupon* and *Living-Social*, then choose a class based on your schedule and interest in the painting. Try to choose something that fits the aesthetic of your home. Consider joining your local studio's email list to find out about specials and upcoming events.

Get Your Hair Done (and Go Out After!)

Getting your hair done is great. The attention is on you, and you get a scalp massage, a chat with your stylist, and sometimes a nice drink. This is mental, emotional, and even social self-care for many moms (if you can leave the kids at home, that is!). But the self-care typically ends when you get out of the stylist's chair. Having freshly cut, colored, and styled hair is such a treat, so don't waste it by rushing back home to your normal daily routine!

Instead of making room in your schedule for just the hair appointment, add in extra time to extend your self-care. Meet up with a friend or your partner for dinner or a drink, or simply head to a café and relax before heading home. For many moms, especially those with young kids, it's a challenge to make the time to wash, dry, and style our hair, so make the most of this time.

Get in the habit of scheduling your next hair appointment at the end of your current one. That way, you'll have plenty of time to coordinate childcare and someone to meet up with the next time you have gorgeous hair. Enjoy!

Take a Hike

While you may want to tell people around you to "take a hike," for this self-care option you're going to take an *actual* hike. Not only will this be physical self-care (be sure to pick a hike that's appropriate to your fitness level and physical condition), but for many, getting into nature becomes spiritual self-care too. Being outside, listening to the sounds of nature, and taking in the sights and smells help you remain in the moment. This can create a grounded and peaceful feeling, which means your hike has become mental and emotional self-care too.

Be sure to research your hike, planning snacks and water according to the distance and temperature, and be aware of when you need to turn around to make sure you end your hike on schedule. It may be smart to invite a friend or loved one to join, especially if hiking is new to you and you're challenging yourself to hike a new trail or difficult terrain. If you're listing reasons why hiking isn't for you (*I don't have the right shoes...I don't have the right backpack*), remember that a hike is just another name for a long walk, one that's often associated with the mountains or woods. But really, you could take a hike at a local park, so don't let your lack of hiking boots stop you. Tennis shoes might be all you need. Hiking can also be a fantastic family outing, so consider if it would work for your family and head out together.

Have a Laundry Bonanza

If you look around your house, how many piles of laundry do you have? You're very normal if you have at least one dirty pile, one clean pile, a folded pile waiting to be put away, *and* several baskets waiting to be washed. You're also normal if you have a load in the washing machine you forgot about. Laundry is an ongoing challenge for moms, because it never stops accumulating. Even if you're not too bothered by the many piles, imagine how good it would feel to have it under control, even for one day.

In "Create a Plan for Your Laundry" in Chapter 4, you created a plan for handling your laundry. The laundry bonanza is about stepping that plan up, powering through the laundry, and getting it *done* (or close to done). So set aside a few hours and get the laundry done. Sort the laundry and start the washing machine. Set an alarm so that you put the load in the dryer right away, then start another load. Have an alarm set for when the dryer is done, and continue to rotate from washing machine to dryer, being sure to finish each load. Fold everything, hang what you need to, and put everything away. Match up socks. Do it all.

For some families, 4 hours won't be enough to get through all the laundry (it also depends on your wash and dry times), but in that amount of time you can get those laundry piles under much better control. And one of the great things about practical self-care like this is that it leads to a better mood and a clearer mind.

Have a Ladies' Night Out

It's up to you how you spend your time with your female friends, but get that social self-care in and do something fun! Head to a trendy new restaurant, visit a comedy club, check out a bar with dueling pianos, or do all of the above. The night might even end up somewhere unexpected!

Planning a night with friends, especially if they're also moms, can be a scheduling nightmare. To combat this, start by suggesting a few dates and asking which one might work best, or choose a date that's far enough out that people have time to plan. You know your friends best, but it might work well to invite more than a few friends because it's unlikely that everyone will be able to attend. Ideally, the other moms have a partner or reliable childcare so that everyone can come. But don't let a few noes or last-minute cancellations get you down. Even heading out with a small group can be a great way to get your social self-care in, and chances are the fun you have will be great emotional and mental self-care too. If you and your friends will be drinking, be sure to plan how everyone is getting home; if you have young kids and car seats, make sure you don't end up leaving your car behind, keeping you stranded at home the next day. Ridesharing options like Uber and Lyft are great choices for nights out like these.

Create an At-Home Spa Session

A luxurious trip to the spa can make for some fantastic mental and emotional self-care. However, there may be time and financial constraints that keep you from enjoying this type of self-care as often as you'd like. So instead of not getting your spa time at all, create your own experience at home! If this self-care activity sounds appealing to you, then you may want to invest a bit of money so that you have everything you need to make the experience as indulgent as possible. For example, you may want to purchase a soft, fluffy robe and a footbath that includes jets. Grab some bath salts, aromatherapy candles or an essential oil diffuser, and face masks and creamy lotions. You don't have to purchase these things all at once; add to your "at-home spa" over time as finances allow.

Plan a couple of hours in your schedule, maybe when your partner can take charge of the kids, or after everyone is in bed. For moms at home with young kids, this can be the perfect way to spend nap time. Make your spa session as relaxing as possible: adjust the lighting, add music, and enjoy. You can give yourself treatments mentioned earlier in the book, like a facial, doing your nails, soaking your feet, etc. You can even get your kids involved (maybe they'll enjoy giving you a foot massage!). Depending on the ages and interests of your kids, they may want to join in your spa day. This can be a fun, bonding experience, too, and could become a family tradition—Saturday Spa Day. Keep in mind that you can do your at-home spa treatment with less time, but for maximum self-care get as close to the 2 hours as you can; 1-hour spa sessions are great, too, but this is meant to be a spa *experience* that you pack with as much feel-good self-care as you can.

Head to Your Local Coffee Shop

You might visit coffee shops often, but most of the time it's simply to grab your caffeine and go! For this self-care option, enjoy your visit and take your time. If you have a coffee shop within walking distance, think about starting with physical self-care, and leave your car at home. Bring a book, magazine, or newspaper with you, and sit and relax. This can become a fun social self-care experience by inviting a friend to join, or maybe you'll run into someone you know and have time to chat! Part of this time can be used for practical self-care. Bring those bills you need to pay, schedule appointments online, or write those thank-you cards that have been on your list. However, be sure to create a mental and emotional self-care experience by enjoying your time, in whatever way you'd like to. Indulge in a special drink, sit outside, or complete this week's crossword puzzle. Use this time to sit, decompress a bit, and interact with the outside world without your kids. Or if your kids are older, consider bringing them to a coffee shop occasionally to do their homework. While they get their work done, you can complete your tasks, or read and get some self-care in away from home for a nice change of pace for everyone.

Drive and Explore

Pick a location about 30 minutes away that you haven't been to before: an outdoor location, a downtown area, a museum, or somewhere with historical significance. The options are endless. Then drive to this new place and explore! Take this trip solo, include a friend, make it a date with your partner, or possibly bring your kids along.

Going somewhere new is generally exciting, providing emotional self-care, and it's mentally stimulating. You could create spiritual self-care with this activity by visiting a church, a place of worship, or another location that you connect with spiritually. What you do at this new place could also be self-care. Find some delicious food, enjoy nature, or simply bring a book, sit outside, and people watch. Including others in the experience adds in social self-care, but remember that it's also nice to do things on your own. Solo self-care can be great if you're around people a lot and need a break, or if you need some time to regroup. If your kids are old enough (or if you can bring a sitter or mother's helper), you can all drive to the location together and then split up for a bit. Though you wouldn't have the entire time dedicated to your self-care, kids often love adventures, so this could be a good activity to include them in.

Hire a Mother's Helper

Mother's helpers can be a game changer for moms, because their job is to help you. Generally, a mother's helper is there when you are home and they make it easier for you to get tasks done around the house. They typically assist with whatever is needed (before hiring, review the tasks you'll want them to do, so there are no surprises). You might hire the mother's helper to play with your kids, which means you can do tasks like getting laundry and dishes done, or your mother's helper might do things like prepare lunch for your kids and sit with them while you clean, taking some stress off of you.

Since you'll be home with your mother's helper, you can often choose someone who is younger than a babysitter, which means the pay rate can be adjusted accordingly, making it a more affordable option for help. Or pay your older child to be your mother's helper. The ages of your kids and the tasks you need help with will also influence the ideal age of the helper. For example, a child as young as ten could be a mother's helper if you want someone to play with your five- and six-year-olds. You might want someone a bit older if you have younger kids, or if the tasks include homework help. If you're not sure where to find a mother's helper, consider who lives in your neighborhood, or ask friends who have kids who are ten to fourteen years old if their kids would be interested. Invite the potential helper over for an hour or so to see how they interact with your kids before making a final decision.

Go On a Date

Regardless of how often you and your partner go out together, going out on another date is rarely a bad idea. It's important that you stay connected with your partner, remember who you are beyond being a mom, and enjoy some time away for this mental and emotional self-care. Though dates can take less time, like the hour-long mini date we discussed in Chapter 6, it's important that you and your partner take more than an hour at a time to connect.

Consider your options for childcare and think outside of the box. For example, plan to head into work late one morning so that you can have a breakfast date after you drop your kids off, or swap childcare on a weekend afternoon with a friend (see "Create and Use a Babysitting Co-op" in Chapter 6) so you and your partner can take a hike or go to the movies. If your kids are old enough, try something like dropping them off at the movies while you and your partner go to dinner. Think back on the types of dates you had pre-kids, before there were restrictions on time or a need for sitters, and try to recreate those dates now. Since dates take time to coordinate, create the time to make them happen, even if they're not as frequent as you'd like. And when the time comes, don't cancel, unless there's a major emergency.

Visit the Zoo

Zoos aren't just for kids (though this can be a good self-care activity to do as a family). Visiting the zoo gives you the opportunity for a fun experience, allowing you to connect with animals and nature and learn a few things while you're there. You'll also do a lot of walking, which means you're getting mental, emotional, and physical self-care in one outing.

Typically, a visit to the zoo isn't too expensive, but there's nothing wrong with looking for ways to save. Some libraries offer free or discounted passes to local zoos, or check deal sites like *Groupon* or *LivingSocial*. You might want to look at the membership options, as they often pay for themselves in two to three visits (and the cost is typically tax-deductible).

If your kids are accompanying you, make sure everyone is wearing good walking shoes and the right clothes for the weather, and has had a good meal before you arrive. You also want to get everyone on the same page about your plan. Let them know that everyone will get to see the animals they're most excited about, plan around any shows or feedings, and decide if there will be any stops at the gift stores. Setting expectations at the start of the trip can save you (some) stress and arguing during your visit. Turn the visit into a full-day activity if you have the time, keeping in mind that many zoos allow you to bring in your own lunch, which can help save money.

Organize Your Closet

If you're like most moms, your closet could use some attention. You might have clothes and shoes that are out of style, don't fit (your body or your lifestyle), and no longer make you feel good. Take the time to remedy all of that by completing the practical act of creating a closet that is clean and organized, and includes only the clothing you feel great about and great in.

When you can see the clothes you have, outfits are easy to put together, and when you feel good in those clothes, you'll be in a better space mentally and emotionally. So take the time to take stock of what's in your closet and create several piles: items to donate, items that need to be fixed, and items that you need to say goodbye to. If you have a small closet, also consider removing seasonal items that you don't need to have accessible *right now*. With the items you decide to keep, hang everything so that the hook of the hanger is backward, behind the closet bar, rather than in front. When you wear an item, turn the hanger the right way, hooked to the front of the bar, as usual. In six months you'll see which clothes you've worn and which ones you haven't. There may be seasonal items, or things that are "fancy," that you'll want to keep, but if a piece hasn't been worn in a while, bless someone else with it. One caveat though: as a mom, you may find that your weight fluctuates, especially if you have a newborn. If that's the case, take the clothes that don't currently fit and put them away, rotating them back in when they fit.

Do Something Cultural

Learning more about your culture, or another, and having a cultural experience can be mental, emotional, and even spiritual self-care. So make it happen! If you live near a city, you likely have many options for cultural events and experiences. For example, look for museums, art exhibits, or celebrations of events like Chinese New Year or Ramadan. You might be able to find a neighborhood nearby that's centered around a culture, like Little Italy or Chinatown, where you can visit, have a meal, and explore the area by yourself or with your family.

If you don't live in or near a metropolitan area, your options may feel a bit more limited, but don't underestimate the power of reading a book, watching a movie or documentary, or even listening to music or cooking a meal from another culture. Involving your children in these cultural activities helps to teach them about the world and people from other cultures, and fosters respect and tolerance. If you have a group of friends with different backgrounds and cultural practices, organize a potluck where each family brings a dish that represents their culture. Get creative with how you bring more culture into your life, but be sure to do it!

Go Dancing

Dancing can elevate your mood, change your state of mind, and, for some moms, feed your soul. Going out dancing with friends can be a very fun social self-care experience. If you're one of the many people who think, *I'm not comfortable going out dancing*, and you worry about your skill level, turn that negative voice off! Remember that dancing is about *you*. Chances are, everyone will be so focused on themselves that they won't be paying attention to what you're doing!

You don't have to have a 4-hour dance marathon (unless you want to!), but consider planning a night out that includes dinner, maybe a drink, and stopping by a place that plays music (live or DJ). You don't need to go to *a club* (unless you want to!). Look for places like dive bars, restaurants that have live music, or even concerts in the park. Many people hear music and they want to move, so you can sometimes find dance opportunities in unexpected places. If you're still not sold on going out dancing, start with doing more dancing at home (see "Have a Dance Party" in Chapter 4). In time you may get more comfortable with the idea of going out dancing, which can be a fun mental, emotional, social, *and* physical self-care experience.

Catch Up on Work

Life is busy. To-do lists continue to grow and things don't get done. Sadly, that's normal for moms. But this can leave you feeling stressed, overwhelmed, and constantly thinking about what needs to get done. You have many roles as a mom, and it's easy to fall behind in one or more areas of life, especially if you're in a busy season. Regardless of the time of year, but especially when you're busy and over-scheduled, it can be useful to put a "catch-up session" on your calendar. With this time you might catch up on housework, volunteer responsibilities, event prep, or even paid work. Though it might not be the norm to bring work home, if using this time for work-related tasks would help you, do it!

Practicing practical self-care by getting caught up on some of the things that you struggle to get done can put you in a better mental and emotional state. Think about it. You won't have unfinished tasks looming over you, or at least you'll be closer to getting caught up. Consider scheduling this time slightly after hours, when your partner is home and can handle end-of-day tasks or on a weekend that's not packed with other activities. It can be useful to get out of the house if your catch-up doesn't include home chores; otherwise you may find that you're easily interrupted. The frequency of these catch-up times is up to you. Monthly may be useful, but it's probably worth it to schedule them in at least quarterly. Knowing that you have a plan in your schedule to get more on top of things can be enough to relieve some of the stress.

Design and Create
a Space That's Yours

Remember before kids, when your living space was your own? You could more easily find things; you had beautiful, delicate items; and you could leave your stuff just about anywhere and it would still be there, in one piece, when you got back. Even if you lived with others, you probably had a bedroom, or at least some dedicated space where you lived that was yours. But moms seem to lose these spaces. Our entire homes often become overrun by kids and their stuff. No more! Design and create a space for yourself that you love. This space could be your closet, a corner of your room that becomes a reading nook, or your bathroom, or, if you can go big, make a She Shed. (Never heard of one? Look up "She Shed" on *Pinterest*! #goals.)

Creating this space does not have to be a big or expensive project. Work with what you have, and create a space you feel good about. Look at what you can use from your home, moving furniture if needed, and visit garage sales, a big-box store, or Goodwill to pick up a few extra items, like paintings, vases, candles, blankets, or anything else your space needs to really make it your own. If you've chosen a space your kids have access to, like a craft table in the living room or a vanity in your bedroom, choose beautiful items that are sturdy, such as canvas paintings instead of framed art with glass, and set expectations for how they're expected to behave in the space. Creating this space is emotional self-care; be sure to use it as part of your regular self-care routine.

Do a Mani-Pedi Lunch with a Friend

Pampering yourself while in the company of friends, without the time constraints you might normally have, is a great way to spend part of your day—and it's a fantastic self-care option. Book a manicure and pedicure for you and a friend, and then follow it up with lunch. Or meet up for breakfast and then head to your nail appointments. Getting extended time with a friend (or two) will meet your social, mental, and emotional self-care needs. Adding a meal in means you're also getting practical self-care too! If you're not in the habit of getting your nails done, this can be the ultimate indulgence. If you get your nails done regularly, adding in your friends and grabbing a meal together can be an extra treat.

When you're at the appointment, sit back, silence your phones, and enjoy each other's company. Consider splurging for additional massage time. Did you know that many nail salons will add on extra time for a massage for a small fee? It's not always listed among their services, so be sure to ask. If they have time, they'll probably be happy to spend more time helping you feel great!

Have an At-Home Date

As parents, we often move dates to the bottom of the priority list. One way to rectify this is to remove the idea that a date has to be away from home. Sure, it's nice to get out of the house with your partner (see "Go On a Date" in this chapter), but that's not always realistic, whether it's because you don't have a reliable sitter, you're not comfortable leaving the kids, or your budget restricts you from paying for a date *and* a sitter. Good news: all of those become non-issues when you have your date at home.

Your at-home date needs to be special, and will probably require a bit of planning. It's not just plopping down together at the end of a long day. Instead, treat this at-home date like you would a leave-the-house date: shower and get ready. Cook if you like, or order in food from a favorite restaurant. Consider setting the table nicely, or have a picnic in the backyard. Be intentional about creating this experience so that it feels like a real date but just happens to take place in your home. Remember, your at-home date doesn't have to be just about a meal. If you love movies, choose one, make some popcorn and other snacks you like, and set the mood for a theater experience. Or set up the backyard for a stargazing date. There are tons of options for at-home dates. Search online if you need inspiration.

Have a No-Plan Afternoon

Between you and your family's activities and appointments, you're probably scheduled to the max. Sometimes it's nice to not have a plan. Remember those days before you had kids, when you woke up and decided what you wanted to do based on how you were feeling? Or plans fell through, and you could just come up with alternate plans? You had hours in front of you and you could do whatever you wanted! Well, now, that won't happen unless you plan it. Ironic, isn't it? You have to plan to have no plans. #momlife. Find a block of time on your calendar, make sure the kids are going to be cared for or out of the house, and just leave the space blank. Alternatively, do this when you can take a personal day at work, or when the kids have activities you don't have to be at. When the day arrives, do whatever you want! You can plan for something to fill your time, like a mani-pedi, but resist the urge to over schedule yourself. Maybe you want to indulge yourself with a visit to the spa, or your mental health care is most important, so you call a friend and unload while you fold laundry. What you do is up to you. See what you're in the mood for, and fill this time with whatever self-care you need.

Work Out with a Friend, and More

Working out may not be your favorite way to spend time, but physical self-care is important. If a friend joins you, not only are you now getting social self-care, but that physical self-care is likely more enjoyable. (If you love working out, it might be even better with a friend.) Keep in mind that your workout doesn't have to be in a gym. Go for a walk, ride your bikes, or bring your kids along in their strollers, but do it together.

Rather than parting ways after the workout, use any extra time for more socializing. Grab a smoothie or juice (at the gym, if they're fancy and have a juice bar), or walk or drive to a coffee shop or somewhere for a meal. You might even go grocery shopping together. Essentially, you're finding a way to get in some physical activity and some extended social self-care. It can be difficult to have only short periods of time with friends, so this is a practical way to get in lots of self-care at once.

Clean a Room

How nice does it feel when there's a room in your house where everything is in great shape? Everything is in its place, the dust has been wiped away, and, even if the rest of the house is chaotic, you have that one room you can enjoy. That's what this practical self-care activity is all about, taking a few hours to get one room in order. It's tempting to try this when your kids are home and you're the only one with them, but don't do it. To really make this happen, your kids need to be out of the house or taken care of by someone else. This is a perfect time to have a mother's helper or schedule a playdate you don't have to be at (return the favor another time!).

Turn on some music, grab yourself something good to drink, and get to work! You probably have your own way of cleaning, but think about putting everything back where it belongs first, then quickly take out anything you don't need or want (donating these items is great, or sell them if you'd prefer), then work on really cleaning.

You may have parts of the room that you'd like to really declutter, like drawers or closets, but don't start there! Remember that the goal is to have a clean room, and sometimes those decluttering projects take longer than you think they will. Though it may seem counterintuitive, clean the whole room and then, with any leftover time, work to declutter as needed, rearrange furniture and décor, or simply sit and enjoy the space. Practical self-care of this kind often helps to lift your mood and improve your outlook, which means you're well on your way to more mental and emotional self-care as well.

Have a Group Dinner

Connecting with friends over a meal can be one of the best ways to get in your social, mental, and emotional self-care. As a parent, you may have trouble coordinating group dinners, but it can be done, and it's worth it to make it happen. One option is to utilize a babysitting co-op (see "Create and Use a Babysitting Co-op" in Chapter 6) and use one of your nights out as a group dinner. (Unfortunately, this means some of your friends would be missing out, but you could do one group dinner a month and rotate the week it happens so that everyone gets to attend, even if it's not every month.) Or choose a date several months out to give everyone time to plan for a sitter.

Or do a group dinner at someone's home. Make it a potluck where everyone is responsible for bringing a dish for the meal. Even though this is an at-home dinner, your kids still need to be cared for, so consider having everyone bring their kids along. Then pool your money and hire a sitter or two to watch the kids in another part of the house while all the parents enjoy a meal together. Even if a sitter isn't available, consider if this group dinner at home can work for you and your friends. It's a low-key activity (unless you and your friends get a little wild!) but high impact for your self-care needs.

Participate in a Sport

Participating in a sport can provide both a physical and social self-care opportunity, and can help to create more positive emotions once those endorphins start flowing. It's also fun to *play*. As a parent, you might be *very* involved in sports: driving, watching, cheering, washing the gear…but when's the last time you participated? Maybe your kids have no interest in sports, and that's kept you from being involved? Every family's relationship with sports is different, but within your family dynamic, it can be easy for *your* interests to get lost or overlooked.

Take the time to participate in a sport that's interesting to you. Maybe you used to play tennis or basketball when you were younger. Check into local adult leagues, or start simply by visiting a local basketball or tennis court for a casual pick-up game. Try something new, like golf, or a solo sport, like running. You can set a goal, like playing nine holes or running a 5K, and work toward that goal, or simply participate without a specific plan. Don't let discomfort about your skill level hold you back; everyone starts somewhere. But if you're feeling a little shy about starting, try to recruit a friend to join you.

Sports can be a family affair (as you know!), so this is an activity you can easily invite your kids to participate in. It can be as simple as shooting hoops or hitting tennis balls against a wall together. If your kids are old enough, another option to get *your* playtime in is to find a location where you can play your chosen sport with them in sight, such as a playground with a basketball court nearby.

Listen to Live Music

There's something so enjoyable about listening to live music, even if it's just one person playing a piano in a restaurant. Enjoying live music is something you can do on your own, with friends, or even with your family, depending on the location and time of day. Where you live, and how close you are to a city or a metropolitan area, may influence how many opportunities you have for live music, but even small towns have options, and sometimes the caliber of talent will blow you away. You might need to plan ahead for a night that includes live music, so consider using your shorter periods of self-care time to research and plan this type of outing.

Regardless of where you live, with some investigation you might find hotel lounges that offer music, open-mic nights for local bands, or restaurants that bring in musicians every now and then. If only the swanky places have live musicians, head out for a dessert or appetizer, sit back, and enjoy. Check your town or city's website and event guides to see if there are any music-based happenings near you, or search online for restaurants or clubs that have live music. You can also use social media to search for events, or ask your friends if they know of any live music events coming up. Even when the type of music played isn't your absolute favorite, the sounds, people, scenery, and possibly food and drink can create a fulfilling emotional and social self-care experience.

Host a Clothing Swap

Have you heard of a clothing swap? It's when friends get together, bring their gently worn clothing, shoes, and accessories, and everyone "shops." The hope is that you leave with some exciting new-to-you items. This sort of event takes some coordinating with the date that you choose, the people you invite, and setting up the event so it runs smoothly for everyone. You want to consider the clothing size of your guests. Chances are, people will bring clothing of varying sizes; try to invite several people who wear similar sizes so they have choices. Consider having people drop off clothes ahead of time so you can get everything organized (like having all pants together, items grouped by size, etc.). Set your home up like a store, have some snacks, music, and a place for people to try things on, and enjoy your time together. Often, leftover items are donated, but make sure everyone's on the same page about what happens to the remaining items.

That's the gist of the clothing swap, but if you want to do more research, search "How to host a clothing swap" online to get more details and information. You could also host a swap for kids' clothing and other kid items. Although you won't get new clothes for yourself, a swap is a great way to see your friends, get rid of kid stuff you no longer need, and pick up new items for your growing kids.

Head to the Spa

Spa visits are a wonderful way to treat yourself. Part of what makes a spa a great choice for self-care is that in addition to getting pampered with the services they offer, like a massage, a mani-pedi, or even personal grooming like waxing, there are often additional amenities you can enjoy. These amenities may include a sauna, steam room, showers, and more, which is why it can be worth it to schedule a few hours to spend at the spa. (Some spas will even sell day passes to use these extra amenities without having to pay for the more expensive services!)

Many spas will have a room that oozes relaxation (think warm lighting, pleasant scents, and soft music), where you sit and wait for your practitioner. You can probably spend additional time in this room before or after your services so that you maximize your relaxation time. Going to the spa provides mental and emotional self-care. Bring a friend with you for added social self-care. Because a spa visit can be a splurge, consider asking for a gift certificate for special occasions like your birthday, Mother's Day, or other holidays. Or look at deal sites like *Groupon* or *LivingSocial*, and check for packages or discounts through spas near you.

Chapter 8

Goals: Activities for a Day (or More!) to Yourself

All the self-care options in the previous chapters will go a long way toward helping you feel more calm, positive, rested, and grounded, and they'll all help improve your overall sense of well-being. However, make it a goal to do more. Pre-kids, it might not have felt like a big deal to spend a day to yourself or to go away overnight. You probably didn't have to wait for the stars to align to take a vacation. But now these things can be tough to schedule. That said, even though it might be difficult (mentally and practically) to make the day-long (or longer!) activities in this section happen, it's worth it!

Taking extended time for yourself is important. It might feel strange and even uncomfortable at first, but pushing through that to the point where you really connect and nurture *you*, not you as a mom, but you as a person, is what these self-care activities are about. Yes, these options will take time to plan, commitment, and support from others to make them happen. And yes, the frequency of these goal activities may be minimal. But promise yourself that they'll happen.

Start with a smaller goal, like a day for yourself, and build from there. Your weeklong trip with a girlfriend may be a year (or more) away, but you won't get there at all if you don't decide it's important and begin planning now!

Send Everyone Out of the House for the Day

There is a lot of self-care that can happen right in your house, but as a mom, you probably rarely spend much time there *without* other people. And if you are "alone," people are usually sleeping or playing somewhere close by. But it can feel very calming to be in your own space, in silence, for an extended period. To help this emotional and mental self-care happen, have your family plan an outing: a movie and lunch, a trip to the zoo, or a visit to a friend's house. Then, once you have the place to yourself, what you do with your free time is up to you!

Take a nap; tackle a big chore your kids have kept you from getting to (like getting rid of toys or old clothes); or just sit quietly, music playing, candles burning, and breathe. Your solo day at home can be a choose-your-own-adventure of self-care. Take a walk, knowing that you'll still come home to peace and quiet; read a book; work on a project; or just do nothing. These activities can happen in small chunks of time, but it's really the longer period of time, the full day, that feels indulgent and special, allowing you to really make yourself a priority in your home.

Go to a Museum

Heading to a museum for the day allows you a quiet space (unless you hit one of those days when there are field trips attending too!) to observe, reflect, and appreciate. Your geographic location will influence how many options you have and the type of museum you visit. If there aren't many choices, don't skip this activity simply because the options you have don't seem like places you'd be interested in. Even museums that don't initially pique your interest can be full of surprises and interesting experiences. Art museums, history museums, and even hands-on science museums can be great places to spend your day. Visit on your own or with a friend. Yes, kids can tag along on this one, but make sure that your self-care isn't lost by inviting them. This mental and emotional self-care activity is a chance to focus on your interests, stimulating you mentally and perhaps emotionally too.

Your local library may give out free passes to museums, so get a library card (see "Get a Library Card" in Chapter 5) and check out their offerings. There may be free days on the museum's calendar, and banks and schools sometimes have discount passes. Keep in mind that there will be larger crowds on the free days, which may negatively influence your self-care experience, but consider all of your options. This is a low-cost, high-return activity. Even if you have local museums, consider driving a bit further to experience something new, and enjoy a meal near the museum with a friend to add in some social self-care!

Spend the Night at a Local Hotel

You've heard the term *staycation*, right, where you basically stay at home and turn it into a vacation? That's awesome, but for moms it's nice to do a "night-awaycation." For this activity, choose a local hotel (probably no more than an hour's drive away) and book a room for the night. Bring a spouse or a friend, or go solo. Just imagine having the whole bed to yourself! Check discount sites online to get deals on a room, amenities like spa services, and local restaurants. Then, once you book, try to get an early check-in and/or a late check-out (or both) to make the most of your night-awaycation. It might seem overindulgent to spend the night away so close to home, but it can be *so* worth it. This mental and emotional self-care option gives you the perfect time to rest and recuperate, and you can layer in additional self-care activities while you're there. This can be a fantastic activity to do for your birthday, an anniversary, or even Mother's Day. Doing this activity as part of a day that celebrates *you* may encourage others to step in and help while you're on your night-awaycation.

Get Your Shopping Done!

As a parent, you may encounter periods of time when a lot of shopping needs to get done. Holidays and the start of school are two typically busy times for moms. You may even have a month that has lots of family members' and friends' birthdays, or an annual event you host. The good news is, you know these times are coming, so you can prepare by shopping a bit here and there. That works well, but it's fantastic practical self-care to just get it *all* done at once. That way, you don't have to continue to think about what else you need to buy, giving yourself mental and emotional self-care by checking these tasks off your list.

Plan a day in your schedule leading up to a holiday or hectic shopping time. This might be several months in advance, depending on how you like to do things. On that day, get everything done. Some of your shopping might be done online. Head to the coffee shop, to avoid being interrupted at home, place all your orders, and then head to the store(s) for whatever else you need. If possible, use any remaining time to wrap and label the gifts.

If you love bargains, start paying attention to sales in the months leading up to events so you can do your shopping at that time. If you need to wait until closer to the actual time, such as right before school to make sure you get the right sizes, still plan a day to get it all done at once. If your kids need to join you and a full day is too much, spread the shopping over several smaller chunks of time.

Attend a Conference

Attending a conference will certainly provide mental self-care, and can also be a social self-care experience, as you'll meet new people. Professional conferences allow you to learn about what's current in your field, hear speakers you admire, and network with other professionals. Personal growth conferences will let you connect with yourself and focus on learning about your own needs and wants. Either type of conference is a great way for you to get away for a day or two (sometimes more) and be around like-minded individuals. And conferences often focus on you as a person or professional, rather than you as a mom (though conferences for moms can be worthwhile too).

Heading to a conference for the first time can be a bit overwhelming, so consider inviting a friend or colleague to go with you. If you're going on your own, remember that many other people will be solo as well, and are likely looking to connect. A great way to start the conversation is to ask where they're from, or what brought them to this conference. You'll find that many people attend the same conferences annually, so think about connecting with the people you meet on social media and continue to interact with them until you attend again the next year. You may meet individuals who become part of your inner circle.

Spend a Weekend Away

Having a weekend away from your kids is a great way to have time for yourself, but also not feel like you're taking *too* much time away from your family and responsibilities. One night away is amazing when that's the amount of time you have, but it's over before you know it. If you can start your time away on Friday night, giving you two nights away, you have more time to settle in, to focus on yourself and what you want to do, and to decompress and reset.

Your weekend can be spent on your own, with your partner, with friends, or with some combination of those people. If you're feeling nervous or hesitant about being away from the family, choose a destination that you *could* return from easily if you were *really* needed. But make sure it's not too close to home, so you won't be tempted to leave for something small. You can also take this time to take a quick flight, or a train or bus ride, and enjoy a special destination.

While you're on the trip, indulge in as much and as many different types of self-care as you can. If you're traveling with someone else, consider talking about goals and plans beforehand so you don't end up hiking when you wanted to relax, or at a quiet dinner when you wanted a night out dancing. Make this weekend whatever *you* want it to be, and most importantly, don't harbor mom guilt. This time apart is good for you and your kids, and can help set the stage for more time away.

Work On a DIY Project, and Finish It!

Finishing a project may be a lofty goal depending on what you want to work on, but with a full day you can make a big dent in a project, and that feels good! Giving yourself time to be creative or work with your hands provides mental and emotional self-care, and it's also exciting and rewarding to create something. With a full day, you'll be able to see *progress* even without completion. If you don't have a project or craft you're currently working on, use a smaller time frame to do some research and planning and possibly shop for the materials that you'll need. Or save the shopping for your project day.

To give you the ability to focus and avoid interruption, you may want to spend this time away from your family, or set your family up with projects of their own. Depending on what you're working on, change up your location. Think about knitting a blanket at your cozy neighborhood café, or scrapbooking at the local craft store. Or, if you're working on a home project, maybe plan an outing for your family so they're not in the way (self-care for everyone!).

You might also be able to make this kind of activity a social event, and possibly a regular occurrence. For example, you could have a crafting circle once a month (or quarterly) where everyone brings what they're working on. If your project can't leave the house, invite a friend over for lunch so you have someone to chat with while you take a break. By planning these large chunks of time to accomplish the things you want to do, you'll walk away feeling accomplished and may be inspired to find additional projects to work on for even more self-care.

Spend a Day with Your (Girl)Friends

Plan a day that is all about you and your friends, where you get together, enjoy each other's company, and just have fun! Your friends, your interests, and your location will influence what you do with your day, but think about visiting a winery together (party bus optional), having a leisurely day of shopping with lunch, doing a mini spa day, or doing something adventurous together, like paddle boarding or a ropes course. The activity you do together will likely be a form of self-care, but the main focus here is social self-care, spending dedicated time with your besties, uninterrupted. The group can be small or large, but invite friends who know each other or who at least know another person in the group so that everyone feels comfortable.

If your friend group includes a lot of moms, consider a full-day itinerary of local(ish) activities so your friends can join for part of the day or whatever their schedules will allow. Depending on the size of the group and the nature of your friends, you'll want to determine if getting input on the activities is best. Or would it be better to decide on a day that works for everyone, and then you take the reins and come up with a plan? Sometimes having too many people involved in planning a day like this can be challenging. Chances are your friends are happy to put a date on their calendars and trust you to come up with a plan that will work for everyone. Keep in mind that there may be one or more people who have to bail at the last minute, so consider this when planning, and remember that you will still have a fun day no matter what.

Spend a Day Being Active in Nature

Take a day to leave your house, get outside, and ideally, unplug. Not only will you likely get some exercise (physical self-care) and enjoy yourself (emotional self-care), but for many people connecting with nature also is a spiritual experience. Your location and what's within driving distance will influence what you do, but consider going hiking or kayaking, visiting the beach, going to botanical gardens, or taking a bike ride and having a picnic somewhere. Yes, these activities can be done in shorter periods of time, but make it a goal to spend the day (or most of it) experiencing nature. Be sure to prepare the items you'll need for this adventure ahead of time to make the most of your day: food, clothing, sunscreen, swimsuit, etc.

This is also the type of activity you can include your kids in. Taking a day to have an outdoor adventure is something kids of all ages love. You could even do a family bonding activity like visiting an outdoor ropes course or having a rock climbing experience with trained professionals. If you'll be including your kids, consider planning the day as a family so they have some ownership over the experience, rather than being told what the plan is. On your day out, set rules for technology use. Go big with a rule like no phones all day, or if that feels too stressful, turn off all notifications and have "phone check" times when everyone can pull out their phones, possibly for 5 minutes, once an hour. Getting into nature and off technology for a while can be fantastic mental and emotional self-care.

Visit a Friend Who Lives Far Away

Do you have a friend who lives *just a little too far away* to see regularly (or ever)? In reality, this friend may be close enough (probably within a couple of hours), but life gets in the way (especially if you're both parents!). Plan a day (or an overnight if possible) to get together. Maximize your time by picking a location halfway between your homes, and meet up.

The distance between you may mean that you can only see each other for a leisurely meal before you have to head home, but it's worth it! Social self-care with a friend whom you don't see often can lead to mental, emotional, and even spiritual self-care, so get this planned. This activity *can* include your kids, but it's probably ideal if you leave them behind. Use your travel time to listen to music you love, an audiobook, or simply enjoy the scenery. This can also be a time to travel differently. If possible, take a train or bus instead of driving. That way, you can use the time to read or even take a nap. You can also plan this as a get-together with other couples that you and your partner enjoy seeing, or a larger group of friends. The point is to stop making the excuse that the person or people are *too far away* and plan a day (even if it's six months from now) to see them and reconnect.

Have an Adventure

What you do is up to you, but take a day (and maybe an overnight) to do something fun, interesting, and adventurous. Kids are optional! For this self-care opportunity really focus on doing something out of the ordinary, something that challenges you a bit. For example, visit an "escape room" with your family (where you work together to solve challenges and escape a room), hike a trail you've never been on, or try a water sport like kayaking or parasailing. (The ages of your kids will influence whether or not you include them.)

By getting out of your comfort zone you stretch yourself mentally, and though you may feel challenged, chances are this adventure will also bring you emotional self-care. Outdoor adventures give you an opportunity to connect with nature and feed your soul, all while giving you physical self-care. Of course, you could have an adventure without the physical self-care, such as spending the day at an international movie marathon, watching a sporting event you know nothing about, or going go-kart racing. There are adventures near and far for every kind of personality, so schedule the day and plan your adventure… or be spontaneous, depending on your mood. Consider if your kids will enjoy this adventure, or if they might be better off having their own adventure for the day, making this a fun date for you and your partner or a good time with friends.

Take a Major Trip

A night away feels great; two nights is an indulgence. So what would five to seven days away from your kids feel like? Ahhmazing! Extended time away from your kids helps you recharge, gives you a chance to reconnect with yourself (and others), and allows you to return to being a mom with new energy. Though you gain some of those benefits with shorter trips, it's important to be able to prioritize yourself and your self-care needs for more than two days at a time.

The ages of your children, your work responsibilities, your childcare options, and your finances will all influence what this major trip looks like, but don't use any of these realities as excuses. Instead, work with them. For example, if you love the outdoors and are short on funds, you and your partner might go camping for a week. If your girlfriend is going through a tough time and you can splurge, maybe you spend five nights with her in a major city.

A trip of this kind takes planning and preparation, so you may need to organize it six or more months in advance. Before you book anything, be sure you have childcare, and find a time when you'll miss as few of your kids' activities and events as possible. Once you get dates confirmed for your kids' care, book something major, like the hotel and/or flights, so that you're committed. You can work on the other details as the time gets closer, fitting in lots of self-care of *every* kind while you're away.

Do a Pool Day

This pool day does not include your kids, because you know it is *not* relaxing scanning the water regularly to make sure all your kids are accounted for (and you know you do it, even when your kids are good swimmers!). No, this is a day at the pool pre-kid style. Bring your magazines, music, snacks and drinks, lots of water, and sunscreen. Even if you don't love the idea of baking in the sun all day, remember that you can sit in the shade, catching up on reading and enjoying some time to yourself. You can add friends for social self-care, but even on your own, a day poolside helps to create much needed mental and emotional self-care.

If you don't have a pool at your house or in your community, check into local hotels or city pools where you can purchase a day pass. There may even be adults-only sections at some of these locations. Even if you have a pool at home or in your community, consider going to a hotel where you can rent a cabana, or have food and drinks delivered to you. It's such a fun and relaxing splurge to be waited on for the day. You can nap poolside, catch up on email, or cruise social media uninterrupted. The pool day is a bit of a self-care grab bag, because you can do all sorts of activities while you're outside enjoying the weather.

Have a Personal Retreat

A personal retreat is time for you when you can tackle the practical tasks that help your life run smoothly, while getting in a bit of relaxation and time for you. Your retreat can be a day away, an overnight, or possibly longer. A retreat is different than a vacation in that there is a focus on getting things accomplished. For example, you could get your meal planning done for the next three months, catch up on the work project you keep having to do after hours, or do some digital organization.

Essentially, you're giving yourself some extended time, away from home, to complete the practical tasks that can hang over you and affect you mentally and emotionally. Yes, you could just do these things at home, but the chances of getting interrupted are high, and that means you won't be able to check these things off your list. Your retreat is also nice because it can include some indulgences. For example, you can meal plan by a pool, invite a friend to meet up for dinner after your day of working, or treat yourself to a movie at the end of the day. During your personal retreat, practical self-care meets emotional self-care and can also hit on other self-care needs along the way. As with your other goal activities, plan ahead for this self-care. Before you go, set aside time and decide which tasks you want to accomplish on your retreat.

Learn Something

Mental self-care and stimulation are always critical for moms, but especially when your kids are young. During that phase of life, you likely spend a lot of time singing kids' songs, reading picture books, and chatting with kids who don't really talk back, or if they do, they're not really listening! No matter what ages your kids are, you're constantly teaching them, and that can get exhausting. But learning is exciting, and learning something new is important mental and emotional self-care for you. So get out there and get to learning!

For example, take a class to learn a new language, take a crafting class to further develop your skills, or do a DIY course. Looking for something more? Take classes to further your formal education or help you develop your career skills. Regardless of what you want to learn, or how you do it (in person or online), chances are you'll need to invest some time in yourself and make an ongoing commitment to your success. Before you commit, be sure to understand the time required. Even for something light and fun like a craft class, you'll want to see it through to the end. And make sure you have support and care for your kids when you're at class. Online options are great because you can learn from your own home while your kids are asleep or engaged in something else. Seeing you study and learn something new is a strong lesson for your kids, helping them see that learning extends beyond your childhood and teenage years.

Conclusion

Being a mom is rewarding, meaningful, fun, exciting, and fulfilling. But it's also hard, exhausting, and emotionally challenging. To experience the positive aspects to the fullest, and to deal with the challenges to the best of your abilities, you need to take care of yourself and include self-care activities on a regular basis. Continue to remind yourself that self-care can be simple and quick, and is truly any activity that helps you feel good. Commit to giving yourself the time you deserve. Aim to experience the emotional, mental, physical, practical, social, and spiritual benefits of self-care every day, even if you don't touch on all of your self-care needs in the same day. Over the course of a week and a month, do your best to fulfill all of your self-care needs as often as it is realistic for your life.

Remember that making time for self-care is worth it because *you* are worth it, but don't be upset if you can't get to it every single day. Even with scheduling and preparing, your self-care plans will be thrown off from time to time. After all, you have kids and a life, and daily surprises come at you. When these things happen, commit to at least 5 minutes for yourself, then try again the next day or week for more self-care. Guilt, shame, and negativity for not doing enough self-care have no place in this journey. Give yourself grace and positive encouragement as you add more self-care into your life.

Remember, the longer you continue with consistent self-care, the better you'll feel; others around you will notice, and you will all feel the impact of your positive changes. Your relationships will likely improve, you and your kids will be happier, and you'll feel more like yourself. So take the time to plan and schedule self-care into your life, like you would any other important appointment. Commit to at least 5- or 15-minute activities every day, 30-minute and 1-hour activities at least weekly, and extended self-care activities monthly or quarterly—more often if you can. And remember, the activities in this book are ideas: try them as is, adjust them to fit your needs and personality, or use them as jumping-off points to find the self-care activities that you love most. Self-care is personal, it's important, and you can make it happen. You are, after all, a mom. You can do anything.

Acknowledgments

Thank you to Jackie Musser, Katie Corcoran Lytle, and the entire Adams Media/Simon & Schuster team. Your support and positivity mean the world to me. Writing this book helped me be more deliberate about my own self-care, so thank you for that. This book captures real self-care because so many moms took the time to share with me what they actually do (or want to do) for their own self-care—thank you for your input. I can't give a huge enough thanks to my friends, who cheered me on as I worked on this project. A big shout-out goes to the boys who made me a mom, and to my hubby for all his support: B, E, and N—I love you!! And finally, to my own mom, I love you. Thank you for everything.

About the Author

For the last decade, as a mental skills coach, Sara Robinson has helped individuals change the way they think and feel to create positive behavioral changes. Sara regularly speaks about the importance of balance and self-care at events and conferences including the Watermark Conference for Women and the Mom Project Summit, and on podcasts like *The SuperMum Podcast* and *The Mom Inspired Show*. Her blog, *Get Mom Balanced* (GetMomBalanced.com), aims to support busy working moms to find balance and time for self-care, and help moms develop the mental skills that they need to thrive. She is a freelance writer and the author of *Choose You: A Guided Self-Care Journal Made Just for You!* (Adams Media, 2018). Sara has a master's degree in sport psychology, is a mom to two boys, and lives in the Bay Area, California.